# Learning to Love Assessment

Jonathan,
Thanks for taking time
out of your busy schedule
to write an endorsement for
my book!
Gratefully,
Sherah

Dr. Patterson,
It certainly is a
small world! Thank-
you for your kind
endorsement 😊
Anya —
7-26-17

# Praise for *Learning to Love Assessment*

"Through historical analyses, syntheses of the latest and most relevant research, application of learning theories, and classroom examples directly connected to teachers' work with students, the authors skillfully reclaim a fundamental part of teaching that has been unduly influenced by federal legislation over the last two decades, reminding teachers of the essential link between learning and assessment—and how they can maintain a love for both. Learning to Love Assessment provides a myriad of classroom-tested assessment practices that teachers at all levels will find useful and can readily apply to their instructional context. The focus on instructive assessment is cutting edge and illuminates practical ways to deepen students' understandings and improve their disposition toward learning. Carr and Bryson provide an oasis of ideas for both new and experienced teachers who are searching for assessment methods to enhance academic performance. This is a book I will use for both undergraduate and graduate courses."—**Kenneth Whaley**, Ph.D., associate professor, College of Education, Northwest University

"Carr and Bryson have provided educators with a wealth of solutions using a variety of assessment techniques to improve teaching and learning. They understand that assessments are a part of good instruction and that teachers need the right tools to maximize information gained from formative and summative assessments. With their practiced solutions, they provide educators with a huge lever that has tremendous potential to unlock achievement gains."—**Jonathan Patterson**, Ph.D., associate superintendent, Gwinnett County Schools, Lawrenceville, Georgia

"A compelling guide for making assessment an informative and empowering process for all stakeholders in an era of high-stakes accountability. With important historical context and numerous examples of 21st-century assessment practices and resources for their implementation, this book is a must-read for educators of today who are committed to facilitating transformational educational experiences for all children."—**Daniel L. Garvey**, principal, Academia de Liderazgo–Universidad Central Del Este (AL-UCE), Dominican Republic

# Learning to Love Assessment

## *Unraveling Complexities and Generating Solutions*

### Sherah Betts Carr
### Anaya L. Bryson

ROWMAN & LITTLEFIELD
Lanham • Boulder • New York • London

Published by Rowman & Littlefield
A wholly owned subsidiary of The Rowman & Littlefield Publishing Group, Inc.
4501 Forbes Boulevard, Suite 200, Lanham, Maryland 20706
www.rowman.com

Unit A, Whitacre Mews, 26-34 Stannary Street, London SE11 4AB

British Library Cataloguing in Publication Information Available

**Library of Congress Cataloging-in-Publication Data**

Names: Carr, Sherah Betts, 1949–, author. | Bryson, Anaya L., 1984–, author.
Title: Learning to love assessment : unraveling complexities and generating solutions / Sherah Betts
    Carr, Anaya L. Bryson.
Description: Lanham : Rowman & Littlefield, [2017] | Includes bibliographical references and index.
Identifiers: LCCN 2017010637 (print) | LCCN 2017028720 (ebook) | ISBN 9781475821406 (elec-
    tronic) | ISBN 9781475821383 (hardcover : alk. paper) | ISBN 9781475821390 (pbk. : alk.
    paper)
Subjects: LCSH: Educational evaluation. | Educational tests and measurements.
Classification: LCC LB2822.75 (ebook) | LCC LB2822.75 .C38 2017 (print) | DDC 371.26—dc23
LC record available at https://lccn.loc.gov/2017010637

Printed in the United States of America

This book is dedicated to all students and teachers with the hope that you will say these words: "I have come to love assessment."

# Contents

# Foreword

During my first few years of teaching, I certainly hadn't learned to love assessment. In those early years, I regarded assessment as an obligatory means to an obligatory end. Like many new teachers, I considered assessment to be one of many inconveniences that inductees to the teaching profession have to go through. Because of the controversies, scandals, and criticisms related to assessment, especially standardized achievement tests, I was skeptical of the uses of assessment for a long time. I was of one of those stakeholders in education that "had come to detest assessment."

It took me years of fumbling through assessments before I began "to see through the fog of negative patterns" related to assessment. Luckily, I had great mentors that eventually helped me view assessment as a tool of emancipation rather than one of hegemony. They helped me realize the critical role that assessment plays in quality instruction. I completely changed my opinion of the value of assessment as I became a veteran teacher. Today, I strongly believe in the power of assessment and evaluation to change the world. In fact, that is my opening line whenever I teach an assessment course.

However, the development of my strong belief in assessment came years too late in my transformation as an educator. There were classes upon classes of students in my early days of teaching that I failed as a teacher; I provided them with subpar instruction because I had subpar assessment practices. Had I learned to love assessment by having a quality text like this in my own teacher training program, that unfortunate situation might not have happened. Therefore, I applaud my colleagues—Dr. Carr and Dr. Bryson—for creating a book that can help generations of teacher candidates learn to love assessment from the beginning of their careers.

In the first two chapters of this text, the authors describe the problems educators and education stakeholders tend to have with assessment. In the first chapter, the authors explain the history of assessment perceptions, from Horace Mann to Betsy DeVos. In the second chapter, the authors explain the complexities of assessment. Unlike many other authors of texts on assessment, Carr and Bryson offer four practical solutions educators can use to solve those problems.

In chapter 3, the authors explain how to create a classroom for student-owned assessment. In chapter 4 (which is my favorite), Carr and Bryson give scores of practical activities that educators can use to enhance their instructive assessment. They provide the reader with before-learning strategies, during-learning strategies, after-learning strategies, and anytime assessment strategies. Examples of those strategies for instructive assessment include Question Dots, the Truth or Lie Game, and the Face-Off Game—all of which can help make school a place of joy *and* learning. In the remaining chapters, the authors provide additional assessment solutions, such as providing active student ownership of assessment and implementing 21st-century assessment.

One of the biggest compliments that my students can give a textbook is when they tell me that they liked the book so much that they aren't going to ever sell it. I'm entirely confident that this is going to be one of those books that pre-service teachers, in-service teachers, and educational administrators will hold on to throughout their entire careers. As readers of this text move from classroom to classroom, school to school, or state to state, I'm sure that it is one book that is always going to occupy a prominent place on educators' bookshelves wherever they go. It's going to be a book that veteran educators point out to younger educators and say, "This is the book that taught me to love assessment. . . . No, you can't borrow it."

Justus Randolph, PhD
associate professor of education, Mercer University

# Book's Companion Website

URL: https://loveassessment.wixsite.com/loveassessment
Passcode for handouts: love2017

Throughout this book, you will see references to our book's companion website. This is a supplemental resource where you can find the hyperlinks to Internet resources mentioned in the book. In addition, all the assessment strategy handouts are in .pdf format on this website. You will need the passcode above to access the handouts.

Let us know what was helpful or any concerns/questions you may have. Please feel free to send comments and/or suggestions to the following email address: learningtoloveassessment@gmail.com

# Preface

"Creativity involves breaking out of established patterns in order to look at things in a different way."—Edward de Bono

We are all aware of patterns. We see patterns in traditions, institutions, even personal actions. This book came about from the recognition of a pattern in how educators were viewing assessment.

Between the two of us, we have been teachers in classrooms working with students for a collective total of 30 years. Our other experiences have always revolved around education, whether as students, instructors, professional developers, leaders, or educational advocates. In essence, we have been living, breathing, and thinking about issues surrounding education our entire lives. We've increasingly heard about the issue of assessment as an area of concern from a wide variety of people at the grassroots level.

We have talked to teachers, parents, friends, and family and have listened to their concerns about the major stress and push for more and more standardized testing in schools. From our perspective, we saw a pattern—that many of those with connections to education had come to detest the term *assessment*, especially when it was tagged to evaluative measures in terms of ranking schools or labeling teachers and students.

The patterns we were seeing and hearing seemed to be a contradiction to our understanding of assessment. The negative aspects of assessment appeared to be taking over the entire narrative. When teachers would speak about assessment to us or to their peers, the narrative tended to be communicated in harsh, negative tones. One teacher commented to us, "I used to love teaching until all these senseless assessment mandates were put upon me and my students."

Our conversations about assessment issues began about four years ago and have blossomed into writing and presenting workshops on the topic. Our goal is to help all stakeholders see through the fog of negative patterns and focus on the positives and creative ways to love and use assessment. We believe classroom assessments—especially in the form of formative and student-owned applications—are the most powerful and untapped ways for educators to develop a passion for ongoing evaluation.

Our hope is that this book will provide encouragement and creative perspectives about assessment. We do not want teachers to feel as if they are defined by outside entities such as federal mandates or test developers. We believe that assessment needs to be viewed as a way to empower students and help teachers be more effective and maximize their teaching potential.

A final pattern that we have heard, especially from classroom teachers, was that they needed to know what good formative and self-assessment strategies look like. Teachers want to improve, but many times they are not given adequate feedback or techniques that help them grow in their ability to be effective teachers. Educators are also seeking ways to upgrade their tools to match 21st-century skills and technological innovations. This book seeks to fill these voids.

In essence, our goal for this book is to diminish negative views of assessment and show educators and students ways to create positive patterns in the assessment narrative. It would be exciting to hear an increased use of the words "love" and "assessment" in the same sentence.

# Acknowledgments

"And always be thankful."—Colossians 3:15

Successful completion of any big project is never a solitary act. This is extremely true in the case of trying to research, write, rewrite, and meet the deadlines that surround the publishing of a book. Since this was our first book, we were also blissfully unaware of the complexities. However, family, friends, and colleagues offered constant support for which we are ever so grateful.

Our deepest gratitude goes to all of those in the realms of education who have enriched our lives and given us the examples and passion to pursue this topic of assessment. First and foremost, we thank the many students whose smiles, charm, and enduring curiosity have given us the impetus to stay with this profession and advocate for improvement.

There are many teachers and administrators in a multitude of schools who have given us insight as to the complexities of assessment. We would like to especially thank our many associates in Gwinnett County Schools and our colleagues at Mercer University in the Tift College of Education.

In terms of refinement, we couldn't ask for a better critic and editor than Teresa Abbey. Her comments about content revisions and the book's central themes were invaluable. Our mutual vision of education was instrumental in helping us refine our words and be more precise in the way we articulated our sense of advocacy.

We are also grateful for the support of our brilliant colleague, Justus Randolph. His work in the areas of assessment, statistics, and data analysis continue to amaze us. We also would like to recognize Jeff Hall and Lucy Bush, who shared their technological resources and assessment tools with us.

In addition to P–12 educators, we are also incredibly grateful to the ideas and challenges of our peers and graduate students in higher education. They have shed light on the issues of assessment from the perspectives of educators directly on the front lines. Their passion for teaching and their responses to our inquiries about assessment have been in valuable.

This book would also not be possible without the process of trial and error. Through numerous offerings of professional learning for teachers we have learned how specific types of formative and self-assessment strategies could be more relevant to teachers and students. Thanks are also due to the Georgia Center for Assessment for its training and guidance in creating culturally and critically responsive assessment stems and for its continued rigorous vision for Georgia's children.

It is a humbling revelation to consider all the people who have contributed to this book. Each one in their own way has added richness to our thinking and application. We are thankful.

# Introduction

"If you don't know where you're going, any road will get you there."—Lewis
Carroll

This book has gone through a number of organizational revisions to seek the
presentation sequence that most effectively articulates our ideas and strategies about assessment. Our hope is that you will obtain content, techniques,
and practical ways to love assessment, especially instructive assessment.
This introduction, therefore, lays out the book's structure and the resources
available to you.

## TEXT PURPOSE AND ORGANIZATION

The purpose of *Learning to Love Assessment: Unraveling Complexities and
Generating Solutions* is to provide educators, as well as other assessment-
oriented stakeholders, with the depth of knowledge necessary to make the
best and most meaningful instructional decisions regarding students. The
first two chapters focus on the complexities of assessment from historical,
political, and mandate-driven perspectives. Together, they paint a picture of
the various players and their perceptions regarding educational assessment.

The following four chapters all focus on solutions. We have had crucial
conversations with educators throughout our careers, which have consistently informed us of the pervasive negative perspectives regarding assessment.
The plea of teachers for more focus on the positive and instructive forms of
assessment was a major impetus for this book. Teachers want constructive
and practical solutions. Therefore, these chapters give concrete ideas for
educators at all levels to increase their awareness and implement effective
classroom assessment strategies.

## Chapter 1: Tracing the Historical Roots of Assessment Perceptions

This book begins with a synthesis of the historical underpinnings of the assessment landscape—identifying where and when assessment became a major player within the international science, technological, engineering, and mathematical conversation.

The first chapter also highlights important legislative mandates that prescribe and monitor assessment as a means of accountability, while exploring burgeoning stakeholder perceptions in response to these mandates. We felt it was critical for our readers to have this historical perspective since there has been a continuing pattern of themes over time—n terms of assessment purpose, design, and accountability demands on educators and students.

## Chapter 2: The Complexities of Assessment Voices and Variables

Chapter 2 extends the identification and description of stakeholder perceptions and reveals the complexities of multiple voices and variables in assessment issues. Readers will explore the role of assessment for key stakeholders—including educational leaders, teachers, and their students. These influential stakeholder perceptions provide an introductory lens into the reasons behind our emphasis that students should operate as the principal owners and users of assessment data.

## Chapter 3: Solution One: Create a Classroom Culture for Student-Owned Assessment

In chapter 3, readers will explore practical applications of assessment strategies, the roles of teachers and their beliefs, and viable strategies educators can utilize to create classroom climates for instructive assessment. Instructive assessment provides a means by which teachers, or those supporting teachers and classroom instruction, can cultivate a classroom environment that supports student-driven data dialogues and instructional decision-making.

## Chapter 4: Solution Two: Focus on Instructive Assessment

Formative or *instructive assessment* takes center stage in chapter 4. There are novel and innovative approaches to cultivate classroom assessments before, during, and after a learning segment. This chapter contains a varoetu of techniques, as well as directions and handouts for using these strategies in the classroom.

## Chapter 5: Solution Three: Provide Active Student Ownership of Assessment

Chapter 5 places the spotlight on ways for students to take ownership of the assessment process. This chapter includes a myriad of student self- and peer-assessment techniques along with step-by-step directions for students and teachers to utilize these strategies in the classroom.

## Chapter 6: Solution Four: Implement 21st-Century Assessment

Chapter 6 embraces the spirit of innovation and concludes this text by focusing on implementing 21st-century methods of assessment—identifying the attributes that 21st-century teachers must possess in order to meet the academic, societal, and prosocial needs of 21st-century learners. Additionally, readers will explore what we label PBL[3], which includes problem-based, project-based, and performance-based learning tasks and assessments.

## SPECIAL FEATURES

In addition to the sharing of literature, research, and strategies about assessment, this book offers two additional resources.

*Pre- and post-reading questions and commentary.* We have created *pre-reading and post-reading questions* for each chapter, as well as personal commentary regarding the questions at the chapter's end. These questions were generated with the expectation of using this text for educator growth in a variety of settings, such as professional learning communities, education courses, book studies, and/or individual personal reflections.

*Book's companion website.* The second resource is the *book's companion website.* All of the assessment solution handouts mentioned in chapters 4–6 are linked on this website and are available as downloads. To access our supplemental files, use this web address and access code:

https://loveassessment.wixsite.com/loveassessment
Access code: love2017

## FEEDBACK AND QUESTIONS

We appreciate and welcome comments and inquiries about the contents of this book. Please feel free to contact us via email at learningtoloveassessment@gmail.com.

*Chapter One*

# Tracing the Historical Roots of Assessment Perceptions

"What we see depends mainly on what we look for."—John Lubbock

## PRE-READING QUESTIONS

Before reading this chapter, it may be helpful to consider your prior knowledge and/or opinions regarding the following questions:

1. What are current perceptions about educational assessment?
2. What is the purpose of assessment?
3. What is the role of assessment?
4. How has the purpose and role of assessment changed throughout the history of education?
5. Is there a need for reformed assessment perceptions? If so, what would that reform look like?

After completing this chapter, you can revisit these questions and review some final commentary from the authors. See the section Post-Reading Questions near the end of the chapter.

## INTRODUCTION

"Don't judge a book by its cover" is a phrase that is often heard when considering initial perceptions. The idea that an external view often doesn't reveal the internal workings applies well to educational assessment. In fact, the term *assessment* is such a loaded word that it has to be unpacked and evaluated in relation to the context and the perceptions associated with it.

Perception formations are phenomena that can occur when experiences or other factors influence beliefs and understandings. The way in which collective perceptions are formed is a topic of wonder to media outlets and the general public. To some degree, perception formations are influenced by information people view online, see on television, read in the newspaper, discuss at work, or chat about with friends or neighbors. The following section will provide information about how the public comes to perceive educational issues such as the role of public schools, standardized assessment, and teacher evaluations.

Researchers Moussaïd, Kämmer, Analytis, and Neth (2013) studied how people form opinions and found that there are two main effects: the *expert effect*, created by the influence of an extremely confident person in the group, and the *majority effect*, which results when a critical mass of people share related opinions. These findings help explain why the public accepts the opinions of individuals who are not experts in the field of education. The findings also explain why alarmist ideas are often readily accepted and frequently pick up momentum, even though they may not turn out to be critical issues in the long run.

Historically, the field of education has been riddled with repeated examples of false crises that generated cyclical trends over time. Some will remember when the Soviet Union launched the Sputnik satellite in October 1957, which prompted public outrage and questions about how the United States could be so far behind in the space race. The result was the collective perception that American schools were failing and therefore needed closer examination of the mathematics and science curriculum.

The media took full advantage of this "calamity," and by March 1958, Americans saw the cover of *Life* magazine emblazoned with the bold heading "Crisis in Education." Today the outcry for further math and science knowledge remains, but it has been rebranded as a new curriculum called STEM (Science, Technology, Engineering, and Mathematics).

For a more recent example of the majority effect, look at how the standardized assessment cheating scandal was fueled by the media, creating a nightmare for all educators, not just those in the Atlanta area.

## TROUBLE IN ATLANTA

*March 29, 2013, Larry Copeland, USA Today*
A Fulton County grand jury indicted 35 Atlanta educators, including former superintendent Beverly Hall, in what prosecutors call a huge cheating conspiracy stretching to 58 schools. The administrators, principals, teachers, and even a school secretary face charges of racketeering, conspiracy, and making false

statements. Hall, who retired before the 2011 release of a state cheating probe, also faces theft charges, because her salary rose with rising test scores on standardized tests.

*April 3, 2013, CNN Staff, CNN*
Investigations into the remarkable improvements on standardized tests were first reported by *The Atlanta Journal-Constitution* newspaper. A state review determined that some cheating had occurred in more than half the district's elementary and middle schools. About 180 teachers were implicated initially. Cheating is believed to date back to early 2001, when standardized testing scores began to turn around in the 50,000-student school district, according to the indictment. . . . For at least four years, between 2005 and 2009, test answers were altered, fabricated, and falsely certified.

*March 25, 2012, John Perry, Heather Vogell, Alan Judd, and M. B. Pell, The Atlanta Journal-Constitution*
In 2008, *The Atlanta Journal-Constitution* broke the first of what would be several stories highlighting suspect test scores in Atlanta Public Schools (APS) and other Georgia districts. In the years that followed, the newspaper continued to dig, eventually exposing widespread cheating in the 50,000-student APS district. The reporting led the paper in 2012 to take on an unprecedented data investigation, which found high concentrations of suspect math or reading scores in 69,000 public school systems from coast to coast. Since the 2012 "Cheating Our Children" series, the newspaper has continued to report on the Atlanta case and test integrity nationwide.

To date, there was nothing more detrimental to the altruistic perception of education than the unveiling of the reportedly nationwide violation of ethics among educators. The actions of a few in the Atlanta Public School system not only injured the reputation of their district but also obliterated the collective calm, confidence, and trust held by stakeholders for *all* educators.

However unintentional, the actions of a few corrupt educators resulted in an erroneous collective sentiment that monetary gain and the public's perception of educational success was more important than making what might have been scant yet honest gains in students' academic achievement. Moreover, the questions that remain ask:

- How did the collective perceptions about assessment get to this point?
- Why were the extemporaneous rewards of cheating a more viable option than a heartfelt attempt to improve students' lives . . . regardless of the test results?
- Why did the teachers, principals, and superintendent believe that their students could not meet the minimum state required level of competency?

For those involved in the cheating scandal, some might assume that the role of money contributed to their calamitous choices (e.g., personnel bonuses, districtwide endowments, or loss of employment). It is also possible that some educators made the decision to cheat based upon their own beliefs and perceptions regarding assessment.

## LESSONS FROM THE ATLANTA PUBLIC SCHOOLS ASSESSMENT SCANDAL

At the end of the day, what happened in the Atlanta Public School system and other systems that resort to those choices was an egregious display of greed, vanity, and self-preservation. Such actions, however, warrant a collective understanding of the assessment fever that seems to be running rampant in 21st-century schools. Perceptions of assessment, whether in support of or in resistance to them, communicate two messages to educators:

- The methods of assessment correctly and adequately represent the body of knowledge acquired by students and are sensitive to the external factors influencing all students.
- Teachers are only as good as their students' test scores.

Although these are, indeed, the messages communicated to educators, until educators realize that assessments serve two functions—(1) to inform funding decisions in education and (2) to inform educators of their students' progress—educators will remain at the mercy of the test developer. It is time that educators take the information obtained from these assessments as useful sources of information, because honestly, they are.

Is it any wonder that the Atlanta Public Schools, which were at risk of closing due to test scores, had educators who perceived testing as an unfair indicator of their efforts? Well, they did.

So what can be done?

To gain a deeper understanding of this phenomenon, it would behoove educators to identify the ways in which historical perceptions of assessment have impacted their profession. An important first step is to explore the history of how assessment has been valued in American society. Understanding assessment history can help educators and stakeholders project a better course for future assessment purposes, roles, and uses.

Take some time to review the following strategic events that brought assessment procedures to their current state. Look for historical examples of the elements of contemporary views about assessment from the following sources: political, stakeholder, international and academic organizations, and parents/guardians. (These views will be explored in more detail in chapter 2.) There is also a helpful table of key chronological events later in this chapter. See page 14.

## HISTORIC LOOK AT THE ROLES AND PERCEPTIONS OF ASSESSMENT IN AMERICAN EDUCATION

The historical path of assessment can be traced back in order to understand how the perceptions of assessment have evolved to such an omnipresent and high-pressured component of education. The history of American education includes traces of methods and tools used to determine ways to measure learning. As history will show, trying to determine ways to quantify and qualify these measures has been a somewhat murky task.

Most can recall visions of the one-room schoolhouse from the late 1800s. Students of all ages and abilities packed into a small building with one teacher responsible for helping children master the "Three *R*s: Reading, wRiting, and aRithmetic." Assessment in these settings followed oral tradition in terms of reciting memorized passages, spelling words, or recalling facts or dates. At the end of the year, students typically took an oral exam covering spelling and arithmetic problems (Sauceman & Mays, 1999).

### Horace Mann's Written Exam

The oral exam as the key tool for assessment started to lose its prominence with the construction of America's first written exam by Horace Mann in 1845. Mann was an educational reformer who pushed for universal public education. A protégé of Horace Mann, Samuel Howe noted that exams could provide "a single standard by which to judge and compare the output of each school, 'positive information in black and white,' [in place of] the intuitive and often superficial written evaluation of oral examinations" (Tyack & Hansot, 1982, p. 35).

Horace Mann also wanted teachers to be held accountable for the quality of their instruction. Mann's own words show his intent for using exam results to expose inefficient teachers or headmasters:

> Some pieces should be immediately written for the papers, containing so much of an analysis of the answers, as will show that the pupils answered common and memoriter questions far better than they did questions involving a principle; and it should be set forth most pointedly, that in the former case, the merit belongs to the scholars, in the latter the demerit belongs to the master. All those abominable blunders . . . [in] orthography, punctuation, capitalizing and grammar are the direct result of imperfect teaching. Children will not learn such things by instinct. They will not fail to learn them, under proper instruction. . . . One very important and pervading fact in proof of this view of the case, is the great difference existing between schools, on the same subject, showing that children could learn, if teachers had taught. (as cited in Madaus & O'Dwyer, 1999, p. 692)

The sentiments in Mann's words seem to echo similar issues today with public perception of assessment and the way in which the community equates testing results with teacher quality. An obvious omission in Mann's writing is any acknowledgment of the prior knowledge or community/family support that students already brought to the examination table.

## Intelligence Tests

Exams became a more popular form of assessment in the late 1800s, permeating secondary schools through the college level. During this time, the existing American universities were concerned about not having a uniform way to determine if students were prepared for college-level course work. In 1890, Harvard president Charles Eliot proposed common college entrance exams. In 1899, the College Entrance Exam Board was formed, and by 1901, the first College Entrance Exam was administered. By 1916, the College Board had developed comprehensive exams in six subjects (Barker, 1967).

Along with the push for written exams at all levels of education, there was a new interest in determining a way to measure the individual intelligence of a child. In 1905, French psychologist Alfred Binet developed a standardized test of intelligence that would eventually be turned into a version of the modern IQ test, the Stanford-Binet Intelligence Test. These IQ tests became hotly debated, and there was concern that if IQ scores were available to educators, there might be the tendency to label a student as "bright" or "slow" based on the IQ score alone (Pulliam & Van Patten, 2003).

Intelligence tests were first used by the army in 1917 to determine placement in rank and type of work. This testing proved so controversial that it was later terminated. However, the classification by IQ was still operational in education. In 1925, it was noted in the U.S. Bureau of Educational Survey that IQ and achievement tests were indeed used to classify students.

David Wechsler, a clinical psychologist, later designed tests that measured both verbal ability and performance of tasks. Intelligence testing remains a hot bed of debate due to misinterpretation or misuse of the results. One of the most passionately contested and researched areas is the cultural bias of IQ tests, which has fueled much educational debate in the literature.

## The Standardizing Movement

Along with the search for ways to standardized intelligence came the quest to standardized achievement. Schools wanted to be able to make comparisons in student learning progress in order to inform stakeholders. Columbia University's Edward Thorndike worked on developing a standardized means to assess student achievement. By 1916, he and his team had developed tests in math, reading, language ability, handwriting, spelling, and drawing.

Going against the opinion of some educators at the time, the National Education Association endorsed standardized testing in 1914. This move was deemed controversial, and some prominent educators such as John Dewey spoke out about the detrimental overuse of *testers* and *quantifiers* (U.S. Congress, 1992). He warned against mechanizing education with a focus of concern on averages and percent.

John Dewey also anticipated the limitations of excessive assessment that focused on evaluation and grading. He believed that these standardized measures could generate an atmosphere of "training rather than education" based on "premature mechanization" of classroom interactions (Dewey, 1922, p. 96). Decades later, Dewey clarified his viewpoints on testing, explaining that

> achievement tests which are used in education are helpful if used to classify students in order to help clarify and promote student growth. If they are used to facilitate a decision that limits options and opportunities for students, that would be counter to the goal of education in promoting individual freedom and social democracy. (as cited in Herrick, 1996, p. 21)

Despite Dewey's original concerns, the standardized testing movement marched forward. In 1929, the University of Iowa adopted the first major statewide testing program for high school students. This assessment later became known as the Iowa Test of Basic Skills (ITBS). This *norm-referenced test* was designed to compare students to other students across the country.

Interestingly, years later in the 1960s, researchers such as Glaser (1963) and Popham and Husek (1969) drew attention to the alternative need for criterion-referenced tests. These tests, in contrast to norm-referenced exams, were specifically designed to provide score information in relation to a set of specific objectives and/or competencies. For example, states used criterion-referenced tests aligned to state curriculum standards to comply with the No Child Left Behind legislation.

Ralph Tyler, who was mentored by John Dewey, conducted the Eight-Year Study during the late 1930s. The research focused on an examination of secondary school curriculum to meet the needs of society. When examining data from college graduates from experimental high schools and traditional high schools, they found no measurable difference (Urban & Wagoner, 2014). In addition, Tyler's study determined the importance of following students on a continuous basis with multiple assessments.

Tyler's study included a battery of tests of general educational competence that would be the forerunners of the General Educational Development (GED) test. In 1942, the first GED test was released, and it gave a second-chance opportunity to many adults without a high school diploma (Allen & Jones, 1992).

As testing programs became more prevalent and sophisticated, there was the need for more efficient handling and calculation of the data. In 1952, E. F. Lindquist developed the design for the first electronic scoring machine. At the Invitational Conference on Testing Problems held in New York City in 1953, presentations were given on issues such as new developments in test scoring machines (Educational Testing Service, 1953).

In 1958, the ITBS would first use computerized scoring and reporting. Testing technology would later advance with the advent of the scantron electronic grading sheet in the 1970s. Many veteran teachers will remember spending hours running scantron sheets through these test scoring machines.

Mandating the assessment of achievement continued along a steady path. In the 1960s, the National Assessment of Educational Progress (NAEP) was established as an ongoing program of testing. Next, the Elementary and Secondary Act (ESEA) of 1965 provided significant federal aid to education, which shaped the necessity to validate the use of funds. The ESEA encouraged states to adopt standards and ways to measure student progress. Thirty years later, the NAEP test was used to evaluate much of the add-on legislation to the ESEA and became commonly known as *The Nation's Report Card* (Resnick, 1998).

## Increased Accountability

By the 1970s, the issue of accountability was beginning to see its first roots take hold. In 1970, Leon Lessinger popularized the idea of accountability in his book, *Every Kid a Winner: Accountability in Education*, with the premise that schools should report gains and failures to the public. This accountability measure gathered steam over time and focused reforms on schools and teachers.

The idea of the focus on higher accountability stakes for teachers was noted by Dylan Wiliam (2010), a distinguished expert on assessment:

> One of the distinct features of these approaches to "testing for accountability" in the United States is that the stakes were much higher for teachers than for students. Indeed, apart from any actions that teachers might have taken against students who performed badly on these tests, there were no repercussions at all for the students. (p. 109)

Along with the accountability emphasis, there was also a push for equitable access to education and for an examination of the root causes of poorly performing students. Case in point, the Education for All Handicapped Children Act (EAHCA) was passed in 1975, requiring free and accessible education for every child. Then, the National Commission on Excellence began gathering data, holding public hearings, and trying to determine the causes and consequences of the educational decline for all students in the country (Urban & Wagoner, 2014).

In April 1983, the sensational report from the National Commission on Excellence was released with the ominous title *A Nation at Risk*. The report indicated that

> declining test scores in reading, mathematics, and science; lessened academic requirements for high school graduation and college admission; and school curricula and textbooks had been "dumbed down" for the benefit of students who were not as capable as their predecessors or their global competitors. (Urban & Wagoner, 2014, p. 319)

This gloomy look at the status of education caused a national stir and varying reactions. For example, two years later, the Council for Basic Education promoted the Back to Basics movement, which advocated that school districts require students with low test scores to repeat grade levels. The high-stakes era of accountability for students had started.

## No Child Left Behind Act (NCLB)

The apex of accountability measures took place with the historical and bipartisan passage of the No Child Left Behind Act (NCLB). Beginning in 2001 and since renewed in 2014, the U.S. federal government signed and reauthorized the Elementary and Secondary Education Act of 1965 (ESEA) via the NCLB.

Within this over 600-page educational reform document resides the seminal components for a multitude of regulations that not only identify the principal owners of data, but also hold these owners (i.e., state districts, local schools, teaching and administrative faculty, and students) accountable for the results that students obtain on national, state, and/or district assessments.

NCLB's regard for accountability, however, is not inherently maladaptive since accountability regulations often work to improve educational equity, professional development, and funding. Unfortunately, even with many of these safeguards, the inability of certain school districts to meet state standards or show sufficient improvement among minority groups has enabled accountability methods to penalize district and local school efforts instead of support them.

## Ten Titles under NCLB

The U.S. federal government determined that the mechanism by which the No Child Left Behind Act (NCLB 2001) would operate would be through mandates designed to cultivate academic rigor and systematic accountability measures established via ten *Titles* of the NCLB 2001 Act. These titles are still relevant under the latest revision to ESEA 1965 under the Every Student Succeeds Act of 2015 (ESSA 2015).

Note that any designation of *former* refers to legislation outlined within the Elementary and Secondary Education Act of 1965.

*Title I: Improving the Academic Achievement of the Disadvantaged.* The primary purpose of Title I under NCLB is to ensure a challenging curriculum for all student populations. The federal government planned to assess the viability of this objective via improved accountability systems (i.e., high-quality academic assessments) that aligned to rigorous state standards.

With the promise of increased grant funding for state cooperation and compliance, Title I effectively regulated the costs and benefits of an assessment-based educational system. Per the provisions of the legislation, each state, in its application for funding, had to design a plan delineating its annual measurable objectives (e.g., standardized assessment, attendance, and graduation rates) in which they would meet the standards for *adequate yearly progress* (AYP). AYP is a designation required in order to (a) prove that local schools and state districts were closing the achievement gap and (b) to secure funding for the following fiscal year.

A second requirement of Title I was that the data obtained via the state's selected accountability system must be disaggregated to illustrate the performance of the "economically disadvantaged students from major racial and ethnic groups, students with disabilities, and students with limited English proficiency" (see section 101, No Child Left Behind Act of 2001, pp. 16–27).

*Title II: Preparing, Training, and Recruiting High Quality Teachers and Principals (formerly School Library Resources, Textbooks, and Other Instructional Materials).* The second means by which the federal government aimed to improve student achievement was through a $3,175,000,000 grant that required teachers and administrators to obtain the distinction of being *highly qualified.* A key caveat to interpreting the definition of *highly qualified,* however, is that the term refers more to the route of distinction, not necessarily one single, solitary measure that educators can take to earn the distinction.

The federal government outlined a 12-part plan that specified the route for states to apply to receive funding in order to comply with the law. The following paragraphs represent a synthesis of Subpart 1 and Subpart 2 of Title II (see section 201, No Child Left Behind Act of 2001).

*Part 1* reformed teacher and principal certification via stringent licensure requirements. The purpose of these stringent mandates was to ensure that all teachers and principals possessed the content knowledge and pedagogical skills to effectively work in their corresponding fields. Through *Part 1,* institutes of higher education were required to produce knowledgeable candidates via rigorous academic standards.

*Part 2* required states to develop and implement programs to support teachers and principals new to the profession by providing the following: (a) teacher mentoring, (b) team teaching, (c) reduced class schedules, and (d) intensive professional development.

*Part 3* required that states develop and implement alternative routes to teacher and administrator certification to facilitate induction of mid-level career professionals who have baccalaureate or master's degrees in mathematics and science.

*Part 4* required that states develop and implement mechanisms to assist in recruiting and retaining highly qualified teachers and principals. These mechanisms include scholarships, bonuses, financial incentives (e.g., student loan forgiveness), and special recruitment of minority populations.

*Part 5* reformed teacher tenure and required testing per content area for certification. Part 5 is an addendum to Part 1 of Title II, which requires teachers and principals to have graduated with a degree in their respective field from a certified institution of higher education.

*Part 6* required ongoing professional development for teachers and principals. The topics of this professional development were to include: (a) improving educators' substantive content knowledge, (b) training educators to provide differentiated instructional methods, (c) providing training to improve student behavior, and (d) providing training to involve parents in their children's education.

*Part 7* made provisions for states to develop evaluative systems to measure the effectiveness of professional development programs that lead to teacher effectiveness as determined by student achievement scores.

*Part 8* required the development of a formal administration within a state educational agency that would report the results of each district to the States' Commissioner of Education and the U.S. Department of Education.

*Part 9* granted funding for licensure reciprocity across state lines.

*Part 10* introduced professional organizations, such as the National Board for Professional Teaching Standards, into the educational marketplace by requiring innovative, research-based strategies to be used as a part of intensive, professional development. These professional development workshops, administered by reputable vendors, would be "cost effective and easily accessible" (Bennett, 2004).

*Part 11* allocated funds to improve teacher instruction via the integrated use of technology into the curriculum and daily instruction and to provide a platform for data collection, management, and analysis. These funds also supported the training of teachers and administrators on how to use these technological systems.

*Part 12* developed merit-based performance systems that would provide differential and bonus pay for teachers who taught mathematics, science, special education, or in Title I schools.

*Title III: Language Instruction for Limited English Proficient and Immigrant Students (formerly Supplementary Educational Centers and Services).* Title III appropriated $750,000,000 to ensure that children who held limited English proficiency not only became proficient in English but also academically proficient to meet the national accountability standards set for all other ethnic subgroups.

In order to achieve this aim, the federal government required teachers to obtain ELL certification via postsecondary education, professional, and other specialized programs. Title III made effective language instruction a national priority via this legislative statute (see section 301, No Child Left Behind Act of 2001).

Title III also brought English-language learners into the spotlight. Through federal grant monies awarded to the Wisconsin Department of Public Instruction, the World-Class Instructional Design and Assessment (WIDA) was formed. By 2005, the WIDA-ACCESS Placement Test was first administered for identification and placement of ELL students.

*Title IV: 21st-Century Schools (formerly Educational Research and Training).* Title IV appropriated $650,000 to the promotion of safe and drug-free schools. This meant the prevention of violence and substance abuse via the development and dissemination of violence prevention programs, uniformed data collection and reporting systems for incidents, school resource officers (SROs), and community outreach programs (see section 401, No Child Left Behind Act of 2001).

*Title V: Promoting Informed Parental Choice and Innovative Programs (formerly Grants to Strengthen State Departments of Education).* Title V allocated funds to states in order to implement research-based programs that complied with the educational reforms thus far outlined within the document.

Such programs include: school choice (vouchers), charter schools, magnet schools, hiring of school personnel (i.e., school nurses and pre-kindergarten staff), counseling and vocational programs, same-gender schools, and community-based academic and health programs. This legislative statute delineated the provisions under which these programs could receive funding and how funding should be governed and described the sanctions for the failure to comply (see section 501, No Child Left Behind Act of 2001).

*Title VI: Flexibility and Accountability (formerly General Provisions).* Title VI, although inundated with details regarding the review and renewal procedure for states to receive grants, the primary purpose of this statute is to appropriate funds to accomplish the accountability objectives of standardized assessment. The flexibility mentioned in this section merely refers to the states' freedom to choose programs that would help them meet the new accountability standards of AYP (see section 601, No Child Left Behind Act of 2001).

*Title VII: Indian, Native Hawaiian, and Alaska Native Education.* Title VII is similar in its purpose to the tenets of Title III: to educate minority or otherwise marginalized student populations within the United States. This statute provided funding for the following programs: (a) remedial instruction, (b) bilingual and bicultural programs, (c) special health and nutrition services, (d) community outreach via vocational training and higher education, and (e) other services to meet the purposes described within this section (see section 701, No Child Left Behind Act of 2001).

*Title VIII: Impact Aid Program.* Title VIII appropriated funding to Warner Public Schools in Oklahoma and Pine Point School District in Minnesota who lost access to funding eligibility because of federal acquisition practices. Title VIII also provided funding to modernize facilities to ease overcrowding, improve access to technology, and provide a reserve for schools to use in the case of an emergency (see section 801, No Child Left Behind Act of 2001).

*Title IX: General Provisions (formerly Title VI).* Title IX clarified the language of titles, definition, and special designations within the NCLB document per title number (see section 901, No Child Left Behind Act of 2001).

*Title X: Repeals, Redesignations, and Amendments to Other Statutes.* Title X repealed previous legislative mandates, including Advanced Placement incentive programs (and funding), certain provisions of *Goals 2000* (e.g., Parts A and C of Title II, Titles X through XII of ESEA 1965), and the *Troops to Teachers Program Act of 1999.* Title X redesignated certain sections of ESEA 1965 and the *Educational Research, Development, Dissemination, and Improvement Act of 1994.* Title X amended the *Education Amendments of 1972*, striking and inserting sections to comply with the statutes of NCLB (see section 1011, No Child Left Behind 2001).

## Comparison of U.S. Achievement to Other Countries

Despite numerous legislative attempts to cultivate academic excellence, as measured by various national and international assessments (see table 1.1), comparative analyses completed in 2013 by the National Center for Education Statistics (a subsidiary of the U.S. Department of Education) determined that the progress made since the clarion call for education reform (i.e., *A Nation at Risk*, 1983) was insufficient when compared to other higher-achieving countries (see table 1.2).

Five international assessments and the years in which they were administered are noted in table 1.1. The United States participated in these assessments, which were designed to provide comparable information about achievement in various subject areas. The tests include the National Assessment of Educational Progress (NAEP), the Program for International Student Assessment (PISA), the Trends in International Mathematics and Science

**Table 1.1.  Summary of Comparative Assessments**

| Assessment | Age/Grade Assessed | Subjects (Primarily) Assessed | Year(s) Administered |
|---|---|---|---|
| NAEP | 4th grade 8th grade 12th grade | Reading Mathematics | Nationwide—annually, since 1969 Statewide—biennially, compared in odd-numbered years |
| PISA | 15-year-olds | Reading literacy Mathematics literacy Science literacy | 2000 2003 2006 2009 2012 |
| TIMSS | 4th grade 8th grade | Mathematics Science | 1995 1999 2003 2007 2011 |
| PIRLS | 4th grade | Reading | 2001 2006 2011 |
| ALL | 16- to 65-year-olds | Literacy Numeracy | 2003 |

Study (TIMSS), the Progress in International Reading Literacy Study (PIRLS), and the Adult Literacy and Lifeskills Survey (ALL).

The PISA data for the United States has continued to raise red flags. The data from the 2015 test released in December 2016 indicated that U.S. scores in reading and science were about the same as 2012, leaving American students near the middle. Unfortunately, the math results were lower in 2015, placing the United States near the bottom of 35 developed nations.

## Increasing Problems with NCLB

As discussed earlier, NCLB created unrealistic goals, especially for schools with large numbers of underperforming student populations. NCLB required states, school districts, and schools to show evidence that all students were proficient in grade-level math and reading by 2014. The pressures to meet these requirements put stress on educators that unfortunately led to unortho-

**Table 1.2. Average Scores of 15-Year-Old Students on PISA Mathematics Literacy Scale, by Education System, 2012**

| Education System | Average Score | Education System | Average Score |
| --- | --- | --- | --- |
| OECD average | 494[a] | Lithuania | 479 |
| Shanghai-China | 613[a] | Sweden | 478 |
| Singapore | 573[a] | Hungary | 477 |
| Hong Kong-China | 561[a] | Croatia | 471[b] |
| Korea, Republic of | 560[a] | Israel | 466[b] |
| Macao-China | 538[a] | Greece | 453[b] |
| Japan | 536[a] | Serbia, Republic of | 449[b] |
| Liechtenstein | 535[a] | Turkey | 448[b] |
| Switzerland | 531[a] | Romania | 445[b] |
| Netherlands | 523[a] | Cyprus | 440[b] |
| Estonia | 521[a] | Bulgaria | 439[b] |
| Finland | 519[a] | United Arab Emirates | 434[b] |
| Canada | 518[a] | Kazakhstan | 432[b] |
| Poland | 518[a] | Thailand | 427[b] |
| Belgium | 515[a] | Chile | 423[b] |
| Germany | 514[a] | Malaysia | 421[b] |
| Vietnam | 511[a] | Mexico | 413[b] |
| Austria | 506[a] | Montenegro, Republic of | 410[b] |
| Australia | 504[a] | Uruguay | 409[b] |
| Ireland | 501[a] | Costa Rica | 407[b] |
| Slovenia | 501[a] | Albania | 394[b] |
| Denmark | 500[a] | Brazil | 391[b] |
| New Zealand | 500[a] | Argentina | 388[b] |
| Czech Republic | 499[a] | Tunisia | 388[b] |
| France | 495[a] | Jordan | 386[b] |
| United Kingdom | 494[a] | Colombia | 376[b] |
| Iceland | 493[a] | Qatar | 376[b] |
| Latvia | 491[a] | Indonesia | 375[b] |
| Luxembourg | 490[a] | Peru | 368[b] |
| Norway | 489 | | |
| Portugal | 487 | United States | |

| Italy | 485 | State education systems | |
|---|---|---|---|
| Spain | 484 | | |
| Russian Federation | 482 | Massachusetts | 514[a] |
| Slovak Republic | 482 | Connecticut | 506[a] |
| United States | 481 | Florida | 467[b] |

[a] = average score higher than the U.S. average
[b] = average score lower than the U.S. average

dox and in some cases immoral behavior, as noted earlier in this chapter. The 2014 goal for 100% proficiency was never reached, and states were offered waivers to be relieved of the NCLB requirement.

## Common Core State Standards and Race to the Top

Two other significant events happened to impact assessment and school accountability. First, in 2009, a state-level effort was made to develop the Common Core State Standards (CCSS) (http://www.corestandards.org). Then in 2010, the Race to the Top competition funded by the American Recovery and Reinvestment Act was launched.

The Race to the Top competition encouraged state submissions that promoted the use of more challenging standards (Common Core State Standards), effective forms of assessment, and data systems to track student progress and evaluate teacher effectiveness. Forty states submitted applications. Delaware and Tennessee won grants in the first round. There were 12 winners in the second round of the competition, including the District of Columbia, Florida, Georgia, Hawaii, Maryland, Massachusetts, New York, North Carolina, Ohio, and Rhode Island (Boser, 2012).

## ESSA 2015

On December 10, 2015, Congress passed and President Barack Obama signed into law the Every Student Succeeds Act. According to the U.S. Department of Education (2016), the purpose of the act is to extend the work of NCLB 2001 in such a way that all students have access to fair, equitable, and high-quality education that functions to close achievement gaps. In order to achieve this end, ESSA 2015 attempts to respond to many of the gaps perpetuated by NCLB 2001 by granting fiscal and jurisdictional flexibility. For example, the act permits:

1. Removal of solitary, one-size-fits-all accountability measures of progress to incorporate several different measures that consider students' projected growth as a measure of students' achievement.
2. Grants and supplemental funding for failing schools versus NCLB's threats of sanctions and state/federal takeover. Government funding is provided in an effort to bring high-quality education to economically disadvantaged communities as a means to prevent generational poverty.

## The Here and Now

As of 2017, forty-two states, the District of Columbia, four territories, and the Department of Defense Education Activity (DoDEA) have adopted the CCSS (National Governors Association and the Council of Chief State School Officers, 2017). These states and territories have agreed to use the CCSS for at least 85% of their state standards.

Since the CCSS place more emphasis on critical thinking, justification, and writing, more sophisticated assessment tools are needed. To meet the demands, former U.S. Secretary of Education Arne Duncan created a federal grant competition for testing organizations to compete for the opportunities to create these assessments. Two organizations won the grants: the Partnership for Assessment of Readiness for College and Careers (PARCC) and the Smarter Balanced Assessment Consortium.

One of the major acknowledged purposes of the new test development was to make better tests, including connecting the most refined measurement theory with new assessment technologies (Brookhart, 2013). It is possible that future exam formats will negate the need for bubble sheets and number two pencils. The use of computers for examination data entry offers new challenges in terms of access and keyboarding competencies. However, some educators express the belief that "testing in the twenty-first century must move beyond evaluating students on the basis of a right or wrong answer" (Ford Lawton, 2014, p. 53).

Currently, the results of reform measures continue to be stale. The most recent state of education report, Quality Counts 2017, by the Education Week Research Center, calculated the nationwide average grade earned for schools to be a C, or more precisely, 74.2. As of this writing, the future of educational legislation and assessment initiatives are hazy since there is some uncertainty about the status of the Common Core Standards and ESSA with the advent of a new secretary of education, Betsy DeVos.

For a more concise view of the key historical elements of educational assessment, view the following timeline of events listed in table 1.3.

## PATTERNS IN HISTORICAL PERSPECTIVES OF ASSESSMENT

Clearly, assessment has played a major role in the evolution of the American educational system. Legislation, corporate entities, and academic experts have all played a part in directing various forms of assessment methodologies and mandates over time. Educators are constantly trying to change and improve the process.

What is curious is that it appears that this constant evolution is turning the assessment process into one of micromanagement. More recent trends seem to indicate public belief in the objectivity of testing and in using test data comparatively and competitively (Brookhart, 2013). The public, in essence, perceives assessment both from the expert effect and from the majority effect.

## QUESTIONING PERCEPTIONS

Before a productive discussion on successful experiences of assessment in all types of educational environments can begin, one must first tangibly define their current perceptions of assessment. Take a moment to analyze assessment perceptions by answering the same questions that were presented at the beginning of the chapter. *Was there any change in perception? Was the perception influenced by an expert or majority effect?*

## POST-READING QUESTIONS

The questions are first listed for readers to contemplate on their own. Additionally, the questions are listed a second time with commentary from the authors' perspectives.

1. What are the current perceptions about educational assessment?
2. What is the purpose of assessment?
3. What is the role of assessment?
4. How has the purpose and role of assessment changed throughout the history of education?
5. Is there a need for reformed assessment perceptions? If so, what would that reform look like?

## POST-READING QUESTIONS WITH AUTHOR COMMENTARY

**What are the current perceptions about educational assessment?** Since the passage of the No Child Left Behind legislation in 2001, we have seen the culture of the P–12 environment steadily evolve from one where

**Table 1.3.   Key Events on the American Educational Assessment Timeline**

| Date | Event |
|---|---|
| 1700–1800s | Early beginnings of schooling opportunities with assessment mostly taking the form of memorized passages and oral recitation. |
| 1845 | Horace Mann crafted America's first written exam and administered it in local schools in Massachusetts. |
| Late 1800s | Urban schools were established with age grading and courses assessed with exams either written or oral. Uniformity was imposed at each grade level through the examination system. |
| 1890 | Harvard president Charles Eliot proposed common college entrance exams. |
| 1899 | College Entrance Exam Board formed. |
| 1901 | First College Entrance Exam administered. |
| 1905 | French psychologist Alfred Binet developed a standardized test of intelligence that would eventually be turned into a version of the modern IQ test, the Stanford-Binet Intelligence Test. |
| 1908–1916 | Columbia University's Edward Thorndike developed standardized achievement tests in math, reading, language ability, handwriting, spelling, and drawing. |
| 1914 | National Education Association endorsed standardized testing. |
| 1916 | College Board developed comprehensive exams in six subjects. |
| 1917 | Army first used intelligence tests (Alpha and Beta Tests) to determine placement in roles. This testing was controversial and was later terminated by the army. |
| 1922 | John Dewey spoke out against the use of *testers* and *quantifiers*. |
| 1925 | U.S. Bureau of Educational Survey revealed that IQ and achievement tests were used to classify students. |
| 1926 | The College Board first administered the Scholastic Aptitude Test (SAT). |
| 1929 | University of Iowa adopted the first major statewide testing program for high school students. The assessment later became known as the Iowa Test of Basic Skills (ITBS). |
| 1932–1940 | Ralph Tyler's Eight-Year Study determined the importance of tracking a student on a continuous basis with multiple assessments. |
| 1942 | The first generation of the General Educational Development (GED) test was released. |
| 1952 | E. F. Lindquist developed the design for the first electronic test-scoring machine. |
| 1958 | Computerized scoring and reporting was first used with the ITBS. |
| 1958 | National Defense Education Act provided federal funds for improving mathematics and science programs and the way they were assessed. |

| | |
|---|---|
| 1959 | The American College Testing (ACT) exam was first administered. |
| 1965 | Elementary and Secondary Education Act of 1965 (ESEA) opened the way for new and increased use of norm-referenced tests and mandated achievement as a main tool for evaluating Title I. |
| 1960s | National Assessment of Educational Progress (NAEP) was established as an ongoing program of testing. |
| 1970 | Leon Lessinger popularized the idea of accountability in his book, *Every Kid a Winner: Accountability in Education*, with the premise that schools should report gains and failures to the public. |
| 1975 | Education for All Handicapped Children Act (EAHCA) was passed with requirements for free and accessible education for all children. |
| 1980 | Council for Basic Education promoted the Back to Basics movement and advocated that school districts require students with low test scores to repeat grade levels. |
| 1987 | Carnegie Foundation founded the National Board for Professional Teacher Standards to provide national teacher certification through a portfolio assessment process. |
| 1993 | The Massachusetts Education Reform Act required a common curriculum and statewide tests (Massachusetts Comprehensive Assessment System). Other states followed Massachusetts' lead and implemented similar, high-stakes testing programs. |
| 1998 | The Higher Education Act was amended and reauthorized, requiring institutions and states to produce report cards about teacher education. |
| 2001 | No Child Left Behind (NCLB) passed and opened the door to the high-stakes testing model and required states to create academic standards to determine curriculum. |
| 2005 | WIDA-ACCESS Placement Test (W-APT) was first administered for identification and placement of English-language learners. |
| 2008 | *The Atlanta Journal-Constitution* broke the first of what would be several stories highlighting suspect standardized test scores in Atlanta Public Schools. |
| 2009 | A state-led effort was launched to develop the Common Core State Standards. |
| 2010 | Race to the Top, a federally funded competition for state departments of education, was launched. It encouraged more challenging standards, effective forms of assessment, and the use of data systems to track student progress and evaluate teacher effectiveness. |
| 2011 | A nine-year study by the National Research Council concluded that standardized tests fall short of providing a complete measure of desired educational outcomes. |
| 2013 | A teacher performance assessment (edTPA) became the first standards-based assessment to become nationally available for use in determining pre-service teacher readiness for certification. |

| 2014 | Partnership for Assessment of Reading for College and Careers (PARCC) and Smarter Balanced Assessment Consortium released assessments for use to align with Common Core State Standards. |
| 2015 | Congress passed and President Obama signed into law the Every Student Succeeds Act (ESSA) in order to extend and fill in the gaps of NCLB by granting fiscal and jurisdictional flexibility. |
| 2016 | Proposed date for redesigned SAT test that will seek to better gauge student preparedness for the rigors of college coursework. |

testing policies and procedures were an increasingly thorny element to one where accountability has become a constant form of 360-degree scrutiny. Decrying the ills of over-aggressive testing has become more commonplace in recent conversations about schooling.

Students, educators, and administrators in all states are confronted with an alphabet soup of national testing demands such as: ITBS, NAEP, CogAT, SAT, ACT, and the newer Common Core–related assessments such as the PARCC or SBAC (see explanation of acronyms at the end of the chapter). Typically, these assessments are enacted without consideration of district-mandated assessments, local school common assessments, and the formative and summative assessments that teachers provide in class. We have expressed concern about how these mandates are intruding on day-to-day teaching and learning (Carr & Bryson, 2014).

**What is the purpose of assessment?** We believe purpose of assessment should be focused on student learning. Educators at all levels should be asking these types of questions about the purpose of any assessment:

- What are students learning?
- What are they not learning?
- How are students learning?
- How are they not learning?
- What can be done to improve teaching and learning?

In future chapters, we will look more closely at how educators can get the focus of assessment back into the hands of students and teachers.

**What is the role of assessment?** If you look at the historical role of assessment, it has primarily served to quantify and qualify the education that students receive in any given educational setting. While this role serves a purpose and sounds noble, it has led to simplifying and even degrading the teaching and learning process. In many cases, the format and content of the tests merely gauge students' abilities to recall facts, proofs, or theorems via abstractly constructed questions set in unrealistic situations. As we will show in future chapters, there can and should be much nobler roles for assessment.

**How has the purpose and role of assessment changed throughout the history of education?** As we have shown in this chapter, assessment has evolved from the one-room schoolhouse level of oral recitations to written exams, to norm-referenced and criterion-referenced exams, to high-stakes computerized scoring and even some open-ended response formats. While the look and feel of assessments has changed dramatically, the purposes of justifying expenditures and comparing student mastery across settings has remained a constant. We have seen other areas of society advance to match 21st-century demands, yet the role of assessment has remained fairly consistent.

**Is there a need for reformed assessment perceptions? If so, what would that reform look like?** This answer is an easy yes. It's one of our key purposes for the creation of this book. Get ready for an eye-opening and strategy-expanding look at ways to love assessment in the chapters ahead.

## WHAT'S NEXT?

Now that the historical aspects and the accompanying perceptions about the purpose and role of assessment have been explored, the next step is to examine the various players in the assessment picture. In chapter 2, there will be a closer examination of these players and how they each reflect a piece of the puzzle in making educational assessment a process to be fully utilized and embraced.

As the book progresses, the case will be made for ways to dispel and transform some of the preconceived assessment perceptions that have been held in both historical and contemporary educational settings. The focus will be on the countless positive attributes and practices of assessment that are underutilized by school leaders, classroom teachers, and students.

### LIST OF ASSESSMENT ACRONYMS USED IN THIS CHAPTER

ACT: American College Testing
ALL: Adult Literacy and Lifeskills Survey
AYP: Adequate Yearly Progress
CCSS: Common Core State Standards
CogAT: Cognitive Abilities Test
ESSA: Every Student Succeeds Act
GED: General Educational Development test
ITBS: Iowa Test of Basic Skills
NAEP: National Assessment of Educational Progress
NCES: National Center for Education Statistics
NCLB: No Child Left Behind

PARCC: Partnership for Assessment of Readiness for College and Careers

PIRLS: Progress in International Reading Literacy Study

PISA: Program for International School Assessment

SAT: Scholastic Aptitude Test

SBAC: Smarter Balanced Assessment Consortium

STEM: Science, Technology, Engineering, and Mathematics

TIMSS: Trends in International Mathematics and Science Study

## REFERENCES

Allen, C. A., & Jones, E. V. (Eds.). (1992). *GED testing program: The first fifty years*. Retrieved from ERIC database. (ED351558).

Barker, D. G. (1967). The history of entrance examinations. *Administration and Teaching, 15*(4), 250–253.

Bennett, J. E. (2004). In search of education's holy grail. *Journal of Industrial Teacher Education, 41*(2), 69–77.

Boser, U. (2012). *Race to the Top: What have we learned from the states so far? A state-by-state evaluation of Race to the Top performance*. Washington, DC: Center for American Progress. Retrieved from ERIC database. (ED535605).

Brookhart, S. (2013). The public understanding of assessment in educational reform in the United States. *Oxford Review of Education, 39*(1), 52–71.

Carr, S. B., & Bryson, A. (2014). Debunking three assessment myths. *Education Week, 34*(4), 24–28.

Dewey, J. (1922). *Human nature and conduct: An introduction to social psychology*. New York: Henry Holt Company.

Educational Testing Service. (1953). Proceedings of the invitational conference on testing problems. New York, NY: ETS. Retrieved from ERIC database. (ED173434).

Ford Lawton, D. (2014). Beyond bubble sheets and number two pencils: Assessment in the digital age. *Delta Kappa Gamma Bulletin, 81*(1), 53–58.

Glaser, R. (1963). Instructional technology and the measurement of learning outcomes. *American Psychologist, 18*, 519–521.

Herrick, M. J. (1996). Assessment of student achievement and learning: What would Dewey say? A "recent" interview with John Dewey. *Journal of Vocational and Technical Education, 13*(1), 17–29.

Kelly, D., Nord, C. W., Jenkins, F., Chan, J. Y., Kastberg, D., & National Center for Education Statistics. (2013). *Performance of U.S. 15-year-old students in mathematics, science, and reading literacy in an international context: First look at PISA 2012*. NCES 2014-024. National Center for Education Statistics.

Lessinger, L. (1970). *Every kid a winner: Accountability in education*. New York: Simon & Schuster.

Lloyd, S. C., & Harwin, A. (2017). Nation's schools get middling grade on quality counts report card. *Education Week*. Retrieved from http://www.edweek.org/ew/articles/2017/01/04/nations-schools-get-middling-grade-on-quality.html

Madaus, G. F., & O'Dwyer, L. M. (1999). A short history of performance assessment: Lessons learned. *Phi Delta Kappan, 80*(9), 688–695.

Moussaïd, M., Kämmer, J. E., Analytis, P. P., & Neth, H. (2013). Social influence and the collective dynamics of opinion formation. *PLoS ONE, 8*(11). doi:10.1371/journal.pone.0078433

National Center for Education Statistics. (NCES). (2013a). *The nation's report card: A First Look—2013 Mathematics and Reading National Assessment of Educational Progress at Grade 4 and 8*. NCES 2014-451. National Center for Education Statistics.

National Governors Association and the Council of Chief State School Officers. (2017). *Common Core State Standards Initiative*. Retrieved from http://www.corestandards.org

Naumann, J. (2005). TIMSS, PISA, PIRLS, and low educational achievement in world society. *Prospects: Quarterly Review of Comparative Education, 35*(2), 229–248.

Popham, W. J., & Husek, T. R. (1969). Implications of criterion-referenced measurement. *Journal of Educational Measurement, 6*, 1–9.

Provasnik, S., Kastberg, D., Ferraro, D., Lemanski, N., Roey, S., & Jenkins, F. (2012). *Highlights from TIMSS 2011: Mathematics and science achievement of U.S. fourth- and eighth-grade students in an international context*. NCES 2013-009. National Center for Education Statistics.

Pulliam, J. D., & Van Patten, J. J. (2003). *History of education in America*. Upper Saddle River, NJ: Pearson Education.

Resnick, L. (1998). *Reflections on the future of NAEP: Instrument for monitoring or for accountability?* Retrieved from ERIC database. (ED429108).

Sauceman, J., & Mays, K. (1999). *Oak Hill School Heritage Education Center: An 1886 one-room schoolhouse*. Retrieved from ERIC database. (ED107431).

Spring, J. (2011). *The politics of American education*. New York: Routledge.

Turgut, G. (2013). International tests and the U.S. educational reforms: Can success be replicated? *Clearing House: A Journal of Educational Strategies, Issues, and Ideas, 86*(2), 64–73.

Tyack, D., & Hansot, E. (1982). *Managers of virtue: Public school leadership in America, 1820–1980*. New York: Basic Books.

U.S. Congress Office of Technology Assessment. (1992). *Testing in American schools: Asking the right questions*. Washington, DC: U.S. Government Printing Office.

Urban, W. J., & Wagoner, J. L. (2014). *American education: A history*. New York: Routledge.

Wiliam, D. (2010). Standardized testing and school accountability. *Educational Psychologist, 45*(2), 107–122.

World Class Instructional Design and Assessment. (2015). *Assessing comprehension and communication in English state-to-state for English language learners (ACCESS)*. Retrieved from http://www.wida.us

*Chapter Two*

# The Complexities of Assessment Voices and Variables

"So, one of the things that people get in trouble with is assessment. It's like a bad game of telephone. Remember the game you played as a kid? What starts out as a perfectly intelligible sentence ends up being some wild distorted thing by the end."—Grant Wiggins

## PRE-READING QUESTIONS

Before reading this chapter, it may be helpful to consider your prior knowledge and/or opinions regarding the following questions:

1. When thinking about the issues surrounding standardized assessment, who are the key players that come to your mind?
2. Of these players, who has the most power to enact change?
3. What are the most crucial concerns of leaders, teachers, and students about increased pressure for achievement gains?
4. In what ways do factors outside of the school impact standardized assessment results?
5. What are some realistic solutions to tackle the current state of assessment pressure felt by school leaders, teachers, and students?

After completing this chapter, you can revisit these questions and review some final commentary from the authors. See the section Post-Reading Questions near the end of the chapter.

## INTRODUCTION

Many educators, as well as the public in general, realize that the current educational assessment system needs repair, but many are not aware of how complex the situation has become. There are a myriad of players in the assessment scenario, as well as multiple variables that impact a school's ability to be successful with the challenges posed by assessment measures of accountability. In chapter 1, the impact of assessment perceptions in addition to the historical roots of accountability was discussed. The focus now shifts to an examination of the complexities surrounding this volatile topic of assessment.

The complex information about assessment in this book is based on a wealth of experience and research, which will illuminate the voices of school leaders, educators, and students, the impact of increased testing, and how microexamination has impacted them. Therefore, in this chapter, the spotlight turns toward the specific roles of politicians, policymakers, stakeholders, school leaders, teachers, students, and the general public in forming the composite picture of assessment. The final emphasis in this chapter will be on examining the variables that affect a school's ability to tackle the scrutiny of high-stakes evaluation.

By developing deeper understandings of the multifaceted players and variables, readers will come to see just how complex and intricate assessment issues have become. Furthermore, it is important to understand that sweeping policy reforms might still not get at the heart of the problems. It may seem hard to love assessment when mandates and pressures have been an amplified part of the equation. However, educators who understand the complexities of assessment will develop more positive perceptions and become positioned to design and use assessments as valuable tools.

## THE NEED FOR POSITIVE PERCEPTIONS

One assumption that all parties must accept is that there will always be the need for some form of assessment tools. People want to know if students are understanding and applying the content that they are being taught. There are also many structures, such as academic standards, international comparisons, and special interests, that rely on assessment tools to measure national educational progress.

Although assessment can have a negative connotation, it does not need to be negative. In fact, the message that needs to be made crystal clear is that *assessment can be a powerful tool for students, teachers, and stakeholders if used primarily as a vehicle for improving teaching and learning*. A move from thinking of assessment as mainly *evaluative* to assessment as *instructive* would benefit all.

To further examine assessment complexities, there is a need to consider all the players in this multifaceted endeavor. Each player approaches assessment with a unique lens. Some of these stakeholders have more power and some have more to win or lose. Ultimately, the player most impacted by assessment strategies is the student. This fact should never be compromised, especially because, as will be shown in future chapters, students can learn how to take ownership of the assessment process.

## OVERVIEW OF STAKEHOLDERS' ROLES

Chapter 1 discusses the historical events and motivations that have made assessment a necessary requirement for the gauge of academic progress. Beyond the obvious progress checks that assessments provide, such as what advancements and changes have been made in order to remedy deficient areas, assessments provide fiscal benefits as well.

According to Lindsay, Hourigan, Smist, and Wray (2013), formative and summative assessment enables stakeholders to ascertain the effectiveness of local, state, and federally funded educational systems and programs. Results from norm-referenced and criterion-referenced assessments reveal to legislators and district superintendents the academic benefit or hindrances caused by such research-based programs as national standards, special education, team teaching, and district-developed assessments.

Research-based programs, however, require funding. Educators must realize that along with funding comes an expectation that those funds are promoting student growth as evidenced by assessment data. This is where the roles of educators within schools are so crucial. School leaders have the opportunity to impact the perceptions of others in the ways that they communicate and share assessment results to stakeholders.

Beyond the political perspectives for assessment reside the perceptions of those invested in the implications of assessment. These perceptions, wagered by such entities as international educational organizations, federally sanctioned or contracted academic organizations, and students' parents or guardians, communicate that assessments are not only a reality but also reliable and valid measures of student learning and teacher effectiveness. Although their voices are an additional source of pressure for educators and politicians, it is important to examine the dynamics of these stakeholders' investment or role in assessment conversations.

## Public/Community Perceptions

An anecdote among educators has been that the public believes that they are experts about schooling concerns since almost all have first-hand knowledge of the situation. Since most members of the public have once been students, they feel qualified to make judgments. However, every person with experience or an awareness of school scenarios in more recent years knows that modern schooling has enormous complexities. Perhaps the 24/7 news cycle or the ubiquitous flow of online information have been partly the cause of this awareness. In any event, the public seems more conscious of the complexities and controversies regarding assessment.

Public opinion appears to be turning against the current onslaught of standardized testing in schools. The 47th Annual PDK/Gallup Poll of the public's attitudes about public schools reported in 2015 that 67% of public school parents feel that there is too much emphasis on standardized testing in the public schools in their community. Consider the changing tide. In 1997, when this same question was posed to parents, only 20% thought there was too much emphasis on achievement testing. Notice the leap of 47 percentage points in 18 years.

The public also seems to be more aware that a test may not always be the best yardstick to determine school accomplishment. In the same 2015 PDK/Gallup Poll, American parents indicated that a better way to measure school success is not through achievement tests, but by whether students are engaged with their classwork and feel hopeful about the future. One could argue that these qualitative goals are hard to measure, but the data do illuminate public thinking about alternatives.

## Political/Legislative Impact

It has been said that "everything is political," and this holds particular relevance when discussing assessment. Joel Spring (2011) described the role of assessment in politics as a means of managing human capital. With billions of dollars invested in salaries, benefits, instructional resources, and physical structures, it is understandable that the governing bodies doling out such funds require a means by which to measure the effectiveness of their investments (Spring, 2011). Unfortunately, however, herein lies the dilemma: just what, exactly, would be the most informative yet efficient method to determine educational effectiveness? The answer: some form of summative measure, or *assessment*, which often seems to be overwhelmingly influenced by politics and legislation.

Because there exists an abundance of literature regarding the creation and evaluation of assessments, test developers (and test-developing companies) have at their fingertips a means to create assessments that are rigorous yet sensitive enough to quantify the approximate amount of knowledge gained by students from year to year. Therefore, because assessment is a viable cost- and labor-efficient means to ascertain student knowledge, it is the method of choice for the business of education. In essence, assessment becomes a form of quality control, especially in the eyes of federal and state departments of education.

As previously outlined in chapter 1, the concept and use of assessment data to gauge academic progress are not new to the educational milieu. The more recent use of data to serve as the precursor to legislative mandates and sanctions, however, is. Similar to NCLB 2001, the principal owners of achievement data are still state departments of education, local school systems/districts, and the local school faculty and support staff, as evidenced by the following revisions:

1. Change from national standards to College and Career Readiness Standards for which state boards of education would develop innovative assessments;
2. Increase teacher observations and evaluations, which include student surveys;
3. Implement competitively based programs, including those employed within charter schools, aimed at raising students' achievement data and closing achievement gaps (ESSA, 2015).

## Policymakers

Educational policymakers have consistently relied on test data to measure the effectiveness of reforms, initiatives, and educators to improve schooling. The perspective that most of these stakeholders have is that concrete evidence is needed to show whether progress is being made and how that progress impacts various subgroups of students.

There have been a variety of yardsticks created by policymakers to measure these goals for assessment outcomes and to report the "winners" and "losers." What is not consistent in these scenarios is the actual validity in terms of aligning assessment policies to learning beyond just language arts and mathematics. Assessment policies should be in alignment with equitable measurement strategies that determine the broad scope of college and career readiness, dispositions, and thinking skills for future student success.

Historically, policymakers have perceived the need for assessments without full realization of how to employ multiple assessments to get at a more multifaceted view of student progress. It seems like cost, special interests, politics, technology expertise, and a basic lack of understanding of 21st-century skills have all added to the roadblocks to assessment reform.

To compound the issue of reform, teachers are often left out of the process. A cursory look at the composition of most legislative or educational policy-making groups reveal a scant number of teachers in the membership. According to the 2014 Primary Sources survey of over 22,000 teachers, educators feel left out of the policy-making process:

> Only one in 20 teachers said they were being heard statewide, and one in 50 teachers felt they had a voice nationally. It would be tough to find a profession facing greater scrutiny by policymakers at every level than what teachers currently experience, which makes it notable that so many of them perceive themselves as not being heard at the levels where most of the major policy decisions are made. (Richmond, 2014, para. 3)

In addition to teacher omission from the process, the actual content and test administration method needs improvement. In 2015, David Conley's research regarding educational assessment concluded with specific recommendations to policymakers to move assessment reform forward. He specifically stressed the need for additional comprehensive technological accountability systems that assess more complex thinking and learning skills.

Along with renovating assessment systems, policymakers will need to look at the entire learning process and how assessment is happening long before summative tools are employed. An evaluation of this process will include the assessment readiness of schools in diverse socioeconomic and cultural settings. (For more specifics on assessment readiness, see chapter 6.)

## International Educational Organizations

Another stakeholder category includes international educational organizations such as the Organization for Economic Cooperation and Development (OECD), the International Education Agency (IEA), and the National Center for Education Statistics (NCES), which exist to create assessments, employ assessments, or analyze international assessments to make comparative evaluations. The OECD is responsible for assessments such as the highly regarded Program for International Student Achievement (PISA) that measures the reading, math, and science literacy of each nation's 15-year-old student population (Kelly et al., 2013).

IEA is responsible for the Progress in International Reading Literacy Study (PIRLS) and Trends in International Mathematics and Science Study (TIMSS) assessments, while the NCES, a subsidiary of the U.S. Department of Education, reports the results and makes comparative evaluations of the United States' performance (NCES, 2013; Provasnik et al., 2012). As detailed in chapter 1, the results of these international assessments help to create the *expert effect* on the perceptions of how the United States rates in education as compared to other nations.

## Academic Organizations

Examples of academic organizations include the National Council of Teachers of Mathematics (NCTM), the National Science Teachers Association (NSTE), and the National Council of Teachers of English (NCTE). These organizations use the results of national and international assessments to create the academic standards, which guide many of the reform referenda of the 20th and 21st centuries (Naumann, 2005; Turgut, 2013). Once again, these are good examples of the way that stakeholders *within* educational organizations impact the cycle of curriculum and assessment change.

## Parents and Guardians

Parents and guardians use both formative and summative assessment results to make determinations of their child's progress along the academic continuum. However, on rare occasions, they also use the results of assessments to gauge whether the local school has done its job in preparing their child(ren) for the assessments and for life.

When parents and guardians perceive the school's role or the function of education as the entity that prepares students for life, assessment results can then become the impetus for real estate depression or expansion, as low-performing schools experience a decline and high-performing schools experience an incline in student enrollment. Therefore, stakeholder perceptions of assessment results can result in assessment having a powerful impact on parents and guardians.

*Try This!* Log on to a favorite real estate website or call a realtor. Look at the marketing techniques per price point. Observe the economic trend for schools that excel on standardized assessments when compared with schools that do not.

## ASSESSMENT ROLE OF EDUCATIONAL LEADERS

The insistence by policymakers and stakeholders that educators be held accountable for student achievement gains has resulted in noticeable shifts in the roles and responsibilities of educational leaders. Fink (2016) reports that "resistance and frustration over standardized assessments and learning standards may have reached critical mass" (p. 46).

The stakes to maintain high levels of student achievement on standardized tests is a concern for most leaders and impacts a large percentage of the way they are evaluated. Some educational leadership organizations, such as New Leaders for New Schools, recommend that principal evaluation systems should place 70% of their weight on the capacity of principals to increase student achievement.

Although not all leaders have this expected criterion, school administrators all know that much of their job security rises and falls on their students' assessment performance. There is the additional pressure that if their school's test scores are consistently low, their jobs might be *reconstituted* by their state department of education.

On the positive side, accountability measures encourage school leaders to have a laser-like focus on student learning. Principals must analyze the rigor of the curriculum, the quality of instructional practices, and stay on top of current data to determine the need for professional learning.

## Leader Voices from the Field

Evidence has been gathered from a wide variety of leadership sources, including P–12 leaders, students in instructional leadership courses, and an abundance of interactions with educators from around the country through workshops and conference participation. In addition, interview data have been gathered that have generated a composite of apprehensions that leaders voice about the increasing pressures and demands from local, state, and federal agencies related to standardized testing. What follows are the themes related to major concerns reported by these leaders.

**Increased scrutiny and accountability.** Ask school leaders and they will overwhelmingly agree that the quantity of testing has increased. In a 2015 survey by the Council of the Great City Schools, it was determined that students in the 66 districts were required to take an average of 112 standardized tests between pre-K and grade 12. This increased level of assessment creates stress on students and teachers, which in turn filters onto the lap of school leaders.

One principal expressed his school's constant assessment scrutiny this way: "The constant examination of how students and teachers are performing on tests is exhausting. It's like there is a constant 360-degree examination of data. It's hard to ever get a break from it all" (Personal communication via an interview with a middle school principal, 2016).

**Finding balance.** Many school leaders talk about the need to find balance in the types of assessments used at their schools. Most principals want to move from an increased emphasis on summative assessments and incorporate more formative assessment, but they also know that school ratings as well as their personal evaluations are based on standardized exam results. As one principal bluntly explained, "Parents and community members aren't coming in to see formative assessment. They are more interested in checking out our school's ranking online" (Personal communication via an interview with an elementary school principal, 2016).

**Supporting teachers.** School leaders, and especially instructional coaches, report that one of the biggest challenges they face relates to the pressures of testing and the need to focus on ways to provide training and support for teachers. One school leader with a large percentage of high-risk students talked about ways that she has shifted from a test-prep mentality. She explains the way she talks directly to teachers:

> What are you doing in class to prepare children every day? How are you shifting your focus from getting ready for a test to what are you doing every day to move the child? Where do you see them and how are they moving? Understand that progress is more important than achievement. (Personal communication via an interview with principal in P–5 school, 2016)

**Focus on evaluating growth.** In interviews with principals it was noted that some leaders had a strong emphasis on helping students focus on the skills they *possess* not on the skills they *lack*. This is not to say there isn't a focus on moving forward. One principal articulated the concept this way:

> If you have an assessment, particularly for children who are from poverty or having issues at home—if it's only about "pass" or "fail," they will continue to have a very low self-efficacy of themselves and they're going to give up quicker. They're not going to be interested in school so I have to give them a "growth" mindset. (Personal communication via an interview with inner city principal, 2016)

School leaders are under intense scrutiny and face increased levels of accountability. Their roles are so multifaceted that it is a chaotic process to untangle. The pace of change and revolving expectations keep school leaders in a constant whirlwind of initiatives and shifting demands. These ideas point to a theory of educational leadership based on the concept of chaos (Sungaila, 1990). It seems that today's school leaders need to be able to function in a constant state of change and possess the flexibility to deal with unanticipated demands at every turn in the road.

## ASSESSMENT ROLE OF TEACHERS

There is nothing more futile than a teacher designing classroom instruction without a gauge by which to measure student progress. Therein lies the benefit of assessment. Assessment allows teachers to develop instructional plans that are rigorous and that align to their state's and the nation's academic standards.

Although some educators view assessment as a structure that limits or otherwise prescribes their instruction, assessment can serve as an informative guide. Educators like to know if they are hitting the mark, and learning targets and assessment data provides that focus. Within this framework, teachers can still employ instructional creativity and freedom, provided the creative experiences help students meet the academic knowledge and skills.

In order to appreciate the benefits of assessment, teachers need a much more comprehensive vision of assessment. Assessment is not a single function; it is happening continuously from their first glance at students at the beginning of the day to the closing bell. Teachers must be on constant guard to assess the learning context, readiness, and acquisition of content knowledge. Teachers can learn to love assessment when they fully embrace its powerful capacity and utilize assessment for *instruction* rather than *evaluation*. (See more on these concepts in future chapters.)

## Teacher Voices from the Field

Although there are obviously many benefits from assessment, many teachers still have valid concerns about the current state of affairs. Over the years, the authors have been classroom teachers or taught, supervised, and/or observed a countless number of teachers in pre-K to high school settings. They have witnessed a profound change in teacher attitude and enjoyment of the instructional process.

For over four years, they have gathered informal surveys from teachers taking graduate courses. One question on the survey is: *What do you perceive to be your greatest frustration as an educator?* Without fail, the overwhelming response continues to be related to the increased pressure and demands of standardized testing. What follows are some themes that have emerged from the literature, research, and personal encounters with teachers regarding issues related to testing.

**Increased stress and pressure to perform.** According to an NEA 2014 survey of teachers, a majority of teachers reported feeling considerable pressure to improve test scores (Walker, 2014). Seventy-two percent replied that they felt moderate or extreme pressure from both school and district administrators to have students perform well on exams. The pressure was so great that nearly half (45%) of surveyed teachers had considered quitting because of standardized testing.

The data have been evident in conversations with teachers who report that testing data dominate school meetings, professional learning, and the school climate in general. Extreme examples are schools where the entrance walls are covered with charts and graphs depicting the teacher's name and test results of each class.

**Pay for performance.** Teachers continue to voice concern about the demands from federal and state entities to have salary tied to their students' success on standardized assessments. Although pay for performance plans take many forms, the most commonly proposed versions flow from flawed logic and several troublesome assumptions. Among the faulty assumptions are the notions that teachers lack motivation, schools are failing, and/or measuring achievement is all that counts (Gratz, 2009).

In the authors' home state of Georgia, tempers have flared and teachers have expressed a sense of betrayal at the manner in which merit pay has been mandated without careful consideration of all the implications. State standardized assessments are not in place for educators who teach subjects such as civics, art, music, or physical education (Downey, 2016). Teachers in these situations rightly wonder how merit pay can apply to them. Circumstances such as these leave teachers feeling devalued as professionals.

**Test score identity.** Another common concern expressed by teachers, especially those in high-poverty and historically underperforming schools, is that the test results almost seem to serve as an identity. When a teacher explains, for example, that they work in an inner-city Title I school, there can be preconceived assumption that they are part of a struggling school with low achievement scores. There can be an automatic supposition that the teacher is part of the failure narrative. On the flip side, teachers in high performing schools feel continuous pressure to maintain a certain status.

The status of many schools can be reflected through all types of media, including Internet sites. For example, there are online school grading sites, such as SchoolGrades.org, that assign composite letter grades that quantify a school's quality ranging from *A*s to *F*s. Educators who work within schools labeled with an *F* may experience tainted perceptions of the school's identity from stakeholders.

**Developmental appropriateness of tests.** One common issue, especially voiced by elementary-level teachers, is that standardized assessments are not developmentally aligned to the cognitive and affective abilities of their students. This opinion has been validated in a 2015 survey by the NEA. The survey found that 70% of the educators teaching the grades and subjects that were required to be tested under No Child Left Behind (grades 3–8 and 10–12 in ELA and math) do not believe their primary state assessment is developmentally appropriate for their students (Walker, 2016).

**More focus on summative than formative or self-assessment.** Another area of teacher concern is that there is more emphasis on summative standardized tests rather than the day-to-day formative assessment that directs lesson planning and efforts at student re-engagement. The heavy lifting of a teacher is the daily self-evaluation of instructional strategies and student comprehension of material through the use of formative and self-assessments. The plea of teachers for more focus on these instructive forms of assessment was part of the impetus for this book. (See chapter 4 on instructive assessment.)

## ASSESSMENT ROLE OF STUDENTS

Assessment can offer students a glimpse into society's value of academic knowledge. In addition to societal values of curriculum content that assessments communicate to students, assessments also clarify the relevancy of academic knowledge to the real world. Many students are aware of the academic content that underpins many of the world's occupations in the 21st century. As a result, students are less likely to ask, "Why do I need to learn this?" and instead are now asking, "How is this skill, which I've been taught, used within the context of a particular job?"

Another benefit of assessment for students is that assessment informs students of their academic progress toward their individually set goals. Students who are taught to interpret their results on assessments can better understand their academic strengths and weaknesses and can develop goals to extend their strengths and satisfy their deficiencies. (For more specific self-assessment strategies, see chapter 5.)

In addition, students who are assessed by numerous types of formative assessment throughout a learning segment will readily have a sense of how they are doing long before a summative assessment. If teachers create environments that help students see their own progression and create numerous opportunities for them to ask clarifying questions, students can take more ownership of the learning.

### Student Voices from the Field

As classroom teachers in a variety of settings over the years, the authors have had the opportunity to gain first-hand knowledge of the ways in which the creeping intrusion of over-testing has directly affected students. The experiences of educators range from sensing autonomy and pure joy in going to a teaching job each day to feeling stress and trepidation from micromanaged instruction and a hyper-assessment climate. What has not changed is the deep concern for students and the support and empowerment they need to learn and grow. One way to support students is to solicit their ideas and empower them to voice concerns.

Capturing student voice is always a challenge. More mature secondary-level students will readily articulate their concerns. Getting young learners to share their opinions about assessment is another issue. What follows are some of the dominant themes that have emerged from years of conversations with students about assessment-related issues.

**Desire to feel prepared.** This concern relates to knowing how to adequately prepare for end-of-year assessments. When a summative assessment covers large blocks of content, students are more apt to forget material. Although content reviews and test preparation can help, course material is often only briefly refreshed instead of taught or remediated due to the vast quantity of curriculum content.

Students have voiced a significant concern about wanting to feel prepared. It is nerve-racking for them to go into an exam and anticipate information on the test that is unfamiliar or far beyond their ability to comprehend. Most teachers have witnessed students sitting idle during an exam because the material is simply too difficult for them to recall, analyze, and synthesize.

**Test anxiety.** Research has indicated that text anxiety for students has risen due to the increased incidence of high-stakes testing (Von der Embse, Barterian, & Segool, 2013). However, one doesn't really need a study to validate what is clearly visible from classroom observation and talking with students. Learners can experience a wide range of stress due to testing. Sometimes it takes the form of physical sickness, while at other times it is the fear of not remembering information or a persistent concern about obtaining the score that will promote them to the next grade, content level, or gifted and other advanced-level courses.

**Impact on self-efficacy.** Because students are aware that it is their own academic proficiency that garners promotion or retention, students who typically perform well in class tend to feel empowered by assessments. Students who have learned to understand the positive purpose and utility of assessment, in addition to their own academic proficiencies, tend to perform incredibly well because they understand that the assessment merely provides a snapshot of their capabilities. Assessment, for these students, positively affects their sense of efficacy because they know that they only need to review the content and that they will reap the rewards of their efforts.

Conversely, those students who frequently experience academic and even social challenges within the classroom are not typically empowered by assessment culture. Students who receive less-than-stellar grades are consistently identified as students who struggle.

Students who require additional one-on-one support from their teachers tend to view assessment as yet another reminder that he or she does not understand, which results in assessment serving as an indicator that he or she is not a productive member of the classroom culture or even society. For these students, assessment negatively impacts their sense of efficacy because their effort does not seem to yield any beneficial gains or rewards.

## COMPLEXITY OF THE ROLES AND VARIABLES THAT IMPACT A SCHOOL'S SUCCESS

After looking at the litany of players and issues in assessment scenarios, it is no wonder reform strategies are so complex. There are a vast number of pieces to the puzzle and some of these pieces can have a domino effect. If one piece falls apart, there is a subsequent impact on the other existing pieces. In an effort to examine the variables of these puzzle pieces, there needs to be a look at the fundamental reasons why assessment reform measures have had a varying degree of success in different school settings.

There has not been a lack of literature and research on educational reform measures. However, what seems to be missing from some of the improvement conversations is a look at why some schools seem *assessment-ready* while other schools seem to be *assessment-challenged*. It is not uncommon for schools to get lumped into categories. For instance, Title I schools may be considered *assessment-challenged* as they appear to struggle to make growth targets.

Absent from these broad-brush analyses is a look at the individual complexities of the variables that might be either causing or impeding the desired achievement gains. It may not be just one or two things, but a complex combination of challenges. To help in this examination, consider some of the following variables that can impact a school's ability to move forward in improving academic achievement.

## Variables That Impact a School's Standardized Testing Results

**Students' assessment readiness.** Studies in the psychology of learning have long reported findings about the benefits of prior/background knowledge in the acquisition of new material. Many schools whose students score lower in academic achievement have larger populations of learners who simply come to them lacking the necessary prerequisite skills. Attempts at catching kids up can certainly help, but sometimes the knowledge gaps and readiness for content are overwhelming.

Beyond academic readiness there are also the social, emotional, and physical needs of students. Students living in poverty or dangerous home settings are worrying more about survival issues than doing well on exams. There is an excellent book on this topic by Eric Jensen, *Engaging Students with Poverty in Mind: Practical Strategies for Raising Achievement*. Jensen illuminates some of the issues regarding struggling students and ways to engage and support them. His techniques have proved successful in helping many schools increase student achievement.

**Teacher experience.** Kini and Podolsky (2016) reviewed 30 research studies that analyzed the effect of a teacher's level of experience on student achievement. They found conclusive evidence that

> teaching experience is positively associated with student achievement gains throughout a teacher's career . . . and as teachers gain experience, their students not only learn more, as measured by standardized tests, they are also more likely to do better on other measures of success, such as school attendance. (p. 1)

The data reiterate what educators have instinctively known: seasoned teachers who know their content and understand the assessment process are assets to student growth.

Unfortunately, many inner-city schools or those with high-poverty populations have difficulty retaining experienced teachers. The pattern of inexperienced educators and low achievement for students is well documented. Fortunately, there have been some efforts at recruiting veteran teachers to these high-need areas. See work done on these issues by Linda Darling-Hammond and Charles Ducommun through the Forum for Education and Democracy.

**Knowing the expectations.** Sometimes problems with achievement gains occur when educators do not fully understand the scope of the test content, the format, mechanics, delivery method, or even the time constraints. As with any academic challenge, preparation is a key strategy. Educators need to be aware of the complexities of the testing scenario. However, this is not a call for additional time for students to perform test preps, but more for teachers to think about how they are scaffolding and reviewing content for their students. Sometimes specific knowledge of the scope of the curriculum can help.

Consider the following example, which provides educators with a lens by which they can determine test expectations by understanding the importance of content domains. In the fourth grade, the Georgia Milestones Assessment System (GMAS) mathematics content area, the five domains of mathematics have differing assessment weights (Georgia Department of Education, 2014). *Operations in Algebraic Thinking, Number and Operations in Base Ten*, and *Measurement and Data* each comprise approximately 20% of the assessment, while *Number and Operations in Fractions* constitutes 30% of the assessment. The blueprint also indicates that the *Geometry* domain only comprises 10% of the assessment.

This blueprint informs educators that while all of the domains are important, stakeholders have determined that for students to be successful in subsequent grades, the content domain of most importance is, in this example, *Number and Operations in Fractions*. Educators can therefore plan their instruction, in accordance to their district curricular calendars, to ensure that students have a solid foundation in understanding fractions.

**Culturally relevant curriculum.** Another concern that teachers have voiced is a lack of culturally relevant examination questions and reading passages. Many times educators cite examples of minority students who are confused by the literacy format and vocabulary on exams. Author Ivory Toldson (2012) expressed the problem more globally: "In general, testing individuals for grade promotion, special education, gifted education, Advanced Placement classes/programs, scholarships, college admission, and employment is a major industry riddled with controversy, debates, and inequities" (p. 184).

It is important that there is emphasis for teachers to teach in culturally relevant ways to support diverse learners. However, some curriculum and test materials have not been updated to reflect the increasing nonwhite population of students in the United States. Teachers interested in advocating for more culturally relevant testing materials can find resources and strategies at The Edvocate (http://www.theedadvocate.org/).

**Timing of feedback.** Teachers persistently voice the complaint that they receive achievement test data so late in the year, or even during the summer, and that they have no opportunity to work on instructional remediation or curriculum scope and sequence. Fortunately, many districts have instituted district-developed assessments that provide interim progress information. These assessments are generally formatted to match the state's summative assessment and, in kind, provide content domain weights as previously discussed.

Some districts have become quite adept at the creation of their assessments so that district-developed assessments can be used to predict students' performance on summative standardized assessments. Note that in the absence of district-developed assessment to measure student progress, educators can still assess students' academic progress through formative measures.

Formative reading assessment systems such as Reading A-Z and Fountas and Pinnell provide teachers with fictional and nonfictional leveled texts by which they can measure students' reading fluency and comprehension throughout the academic year. Mathematics progress assessments can be obtained by a simple Internet query. Some states such as Georgia and North Carolina offer free access to their mathematics curriculum calendars, lessons, and performance tasks. These resources offer a vehicle by which educators can scaffold students' prior knowledge to the curricular standards of learning (see this chapter's references).

**Support systems in place.** Teachers naturally want all of their students to do well on standardized assessments. However, as previously mentioned, there are many roadblocks leading to continued teacher frustration about the lack of support systems, professional learning, and planning time to help them hone their content and/or know how to support a multitude of learning needs.

In turn, students feel a lack of support, whether it be parents who are unable to help because of work constraints, an inability to understand schoolwork, or other reasons that do not indicate a lack of caring. Students can also struggle with problems such as self-regulatory functioning, a lack of relevance in formal schooling, and/or increased punitive accountability.

Most schools have support systems in place, but from the teachers' standpoint, it is still not enough to meet the variety of needs of English-language learners and students with special needs, as well as the additional complexities that today's students bring to school.

Here's where the conversation has to move to looking at the total picture. If school policymakers or macrolevel leaders think legislation and policy mandates are going to fix the problem, they are severely misguided. It will take a much more intimate and personal view of the complexities to pursue effective reform.

## MOVING THE FOCUS TO SOLUTIONS

As this chapter winds down, think about how complex the topic of standardized testing has become. Do not become overwhelmed for there are ways that individual educators can begin to make a dent in the problem. Despite the inherent complexities discussed in this chapter, there are many reasons to love assessment. One key factor than can cultivate positive thinking is to move from thinking of assessment as mainly *evaluative* to seeing assessment as *instructive*. In the next chapter, the focus will move toward solutions and the ultimate goal of possessing a passion for classroom assessment.

## POST-READING QUESTIONS

The questions are first listed for readers to contemplate on their own. Additionally, the questions are listed a second time with commentary from the authors' perspectives.

1. When thinking about the issues surrounding standardized assessment, who are the key players that come to your mind?
2. Of these players, who has the most power to enact change?
3. What are the most crucial concerns of leaders, teachers, and students about increased pressure for achievement gains?
4. In what ways do factors outside of the school impact standardized assessment results?
5. What are some realistic solutions to tackle the current state of assessment pressure felt by school leaders, teachers, and students?

## POST-READING QUESTIONS

**When thinking about the issues surrounding standardized assessment, who are the key players that come to your mind?** Perhaps the initial answer to this question that came to your mind was completely different from the ideas that we presented in this chapter. That's because most perceptions about the players in the assessment picture come from our personal experiences. For example, when we are wearing our teacher hat, we tend to envision the most important player as the student. Without the student, there would be no need for this entire school assessment process.

On the other hand, when we are wearing our leader hat, we might focus more on the players that promote assessment rules and regulations or top-down mandates that dictate the type of assessment and the parameters of the battery of instruments that are going to be used. We might start thinking ahead about how assessment data will be viewed by a superintendent or how our school's ranking might be perceived by the school community.

In any event, key assessment players may be different depending on your frame of reference.

**Of these players, who has the most power to enact change?** Again, this response might be generated from a personal opinion or experience. In our many conversations about assessment through the course of writing this book, we have vented and complained about how powerless we feel in terms of creating systemic change. We have come to realize that there are forces at the state and federal level that dictate the major assessment mandates for the teachers in our state.

As with all large government entities, many decisions are financial in nature. For instance, in 2010, the state of Georgia acquired funding to the tune of $400 million by winning one of the federal Race to the Top grants. Along with the grant funding was the caveat that our state would agree to link test scores to teacher evaluations. As we mentioned in this chapter, the new merit pay mandates in Georgia could cause severe backlash and deplete teacher morale.

Sadly, in education we see that influential players such as politicians, textbook publishers, and testing companies wield a great deal of power. We believe that the old saying about "follow the money" holds as true in education as it does in other professions.

At the same time, we have seen teacher leaders who have been very powerful advocates for students. We believe there are strong educators with the passion and stamina necessary to enact change. Perhaps you are one of them?

**What are the most crucial concerns of leaders, teachers, and students about increased pressure for achievement gains?** This answer also tends to reflect your own viewpoints. From where we sit, our greatest concern resides with the students and teachers. Because we are both actively engaged in educational practice, whether in the classroom teaching students or directly teaching teachers, we have our minds and hearts on the pulse of the educator's struggle in this day and age.

We cannot ignore the fact that we have heard increased cries of concern about how assessment has reached a tipping point in terms of instructional time spent on either test prep or test administration or data analysis. We know that data are crucial to sound instructional decisions, but it seems like the pendulum has swung too far and teachers are now oversaturated with testing mandates and expectations.

**In what ways do factors outside of the school impact standardized assessment results?** This question is one that is near and dear to our hearts. Having spent so many years in the classroom nurturing and listening to student needs, we are exceptionally sensitive to the fact that each student brings a complex set of variables to an assessment encounter. We have worked with students who are living in precarious home settings. Some students are serving as "parents" for younger siblings. Some students have after-school jobs during the week and don't get home until late at night. Other students come to school in the morning worrying more about breakfast than the test review questions.

On the day of testing, many students don't just bring a number two pencil to the exam. Additionally, they bring a whole set of mental and even sometimes physical baggage that impacts their performance. So, yes, the people outside of school settings can sit in their comfortable offices and examine the test scores of our students with deep scrutiny. But many times it's only the classroom teacher who knows the real story of the factors that impact assessment results.

**What are some realistic solutions to tackle the current state of assessment pressure felt by school leaders, teachers, and students?** There are many solutions that we can suggest. Please keep reading. The chapters that follow will offer numerous resolutions to assessment challenges.

## REFERENCES

Conley, D. T. (2015). A new era for educational assessment. *Education Policy Analysis Archives, 23*(8). Retrieved from http://dx.doi.org/10.14507/epaa.v23.1983

Council of the Great City Schools. (2015, October). *Student testing in America's great city schools: An inventory and preliminary analysis.* Retrieved from http://www.cgcs.org/cms/lib/dc00001581/centricity/domain/87/testing%20report.pdf

Downey, M. (2016, January 3). Merit pay for teachers: Is Georgia playing with fire? *Atlanta-Journal Constitution.* Retrieved from http://getschooled.blog.myajc.com/2016/01/03/merit-pay-for-teachers-is-georgia-legplaying-with-fire/

Fink, J. (2016). Push for sensible testing. *District Administration, 52*(1), 46–48.

Fountas, I., & Pinnell, G. S. (2015). *Fountas and Pinnell leveled books.* Retrieved from http://www.fountasandpinnellleveledbooks.com/default.aspx

Georgia Department of Education. (2014). *Georgia Milestones Assessment System: Domain structures and content weights Grade 4.* Retrieved from http://www.gadoe.org/Curriculum-Instruction-and-Assessment/Assessment/Documents/GM%20Grade%204%20Test%20Blueprints.pdf

Gratz, D. B. (2009). The problem with performance pay. *Educational Leadership, 67*(3), 76–79.

Hammond, L. D., & Ducommun, C. E. (n.d.). Recruiting and retaining teachers: What matters most and what can government do? *The Forum for Education and Democracy.* Retrieved from https://pdfs.semanticscholar.org/71af/3a3afb53ec134ecd1a409170d6bacdc2c35c.pdf

Jensen, E. (2013). *Engaging students with poverty in mind: Practical strategies for raising achievement.* Alexandria, VA: ASCD.

Kelly, D., Nord, C. W., Jenkins, F., Chan, J. Y., Kastberg, D., & National Center for Education Statistics. (2013). *Performance of U.S. 15-year-old students in mathematics, science, and reading literacy in an international context: First look at PISA 2012.* NCES 2014-024. National Center for Education Statistics.

Kini, T., & Podolsky, A. (2016). *Does teaching experience increase teacher effectiveness? A review of the research.* Palo Alto, CA: Learning Policy Institute. Retrieved from https://learningpolicyinstitute.org/our-work/publications-resources/ does-teaching-experience-increase-teacher-effectiveness-review-research

Lindsay, N., Hourigan, A., Smist, J., & Wray, L. (2013). Let me be direct: Using direct assessments with student leaders. *About Campus, 17*(6), 30–32.

National Center for Education Statistics. (NCES). (2013). *The nation's report card: A First Look—2013 Mathematics and Reading National Assessment of Educational Progress at Grade 4 and 8.* NCES 2014-451. National Center for Education Statistics.

Naumann, J. (2005). TIMMS, PISA, PIRLS, and low educational achievement in world society. *Prospects: Quarterly Review of Comparative Education, 35*(2), 229–248.

New Leaders for New Schools. (2010). *Evaluating principals: Balancing accountability with professional growth.* Retrieved from ERIC database. (ED532070).

PDK International. (1997). 31st annual PDK/Gallup Poll of the public's attitudes about the public schools. *Phi Delta Kappan, 81*(1), 41–56.

PDK International. (2015). 47th annual PDK/Gallup poll of the public's attitudes about the public schools. *Phi Delta Kappan, 97*(1), K1–K32.

Provasnik, S., Kastberg, D., Ferraro, D., Lemanski, N., Roey, S., & Jenkins, F. (2012). *Highlights from TIMSS 2011: Mathematics and science achievement of U.S. fourth- and eighth-grade students in an international context.* NCES 2013-009. National Center for Education Statistics.

Reading A-Z (2015). Reading A-Z. Retrieved from https://www.readinga-z.com

Richmond, E. (2014, February 26). New survey: Teachers say their voices aren't being heard. *Education Writers Association.* Retrieved from http://www.ewa.org/blog-educated-reporter/new-survey-teachers-say-their-voices-arent-being-heard

Spring, J. (2011). *The politics of American education.* New York: Routledge.

Sungaila, H. (1990). The new science of chaos: Making a new science of leadership. *Journal of Educational Administration, 28*(2), 4–23.

Toldson, I. A. (2012). Editor's comment: When standardized tests miss the mark. *Journal of Negro Education, 81*(3), 181–185.

Turgut, G. (2013). International tests and the U.S. educational reforms: Can success be replicated? *Clearing House: A Journal of Educational Strategies, Issues, and Ideas, 86*(2), 64–73.

U.S. Department of Education. (2001). *NCLB overview: Executive summary.* Retrieved from http://www2.ed.gov/nclb/overview/intro/execsumm.html

Von der Embse, N., Barterian, J., & Segool, N. (2013). Test anxiety interventions for children and adolescents, *Psychology in the Schools, 50*(1), 57–71.

Walker, T. (2014, November 2). NEA survey: Nearly half of teachers consider leaving the profession due to standardized testing. *NEA Today.* Retrieved from http://neatoday.org/2014/11/02/nea-survey-nearly-half-of-teachers-consider-leaving-profession-due-to-standardized-testing-2/

Walker, T. (2016, February 18). Survey: 70 percent of educators say state assessments not developmentally appropriate. *NEA Today.* Retrieved from http://neatoday.org/2016/02/18/standardized-tests-not-developmentally-appropriate/

Wiggins, G. (2002, January 21). Defining assessment. *Edutopia.* Retrieved from https://www.edutopia.org/grant-wiggins-assessment

*Chapter Three*

# Solution One

## *Create a Classroom Culture for Student-Owned Assessment*

"For good teaching rests neither in accumulating a shelfful of knowledge nor in developing a repertoire of skills. In the end, good teaching lies in a willingness to attend and care for what happens in our students, ourselves, and the space between us. Good teaching is a certain kind of stance, I think. It is a stance of receptivity, of attunement, of listening."—Laurent A. Daloz

### PRE-READING QUESTIONS

Before reading this chapter, consider your prior knowledge/opinions regarding these questions:

1. How would you describe classroom culture?
2. What are examples of teachers having asset versus deficit thinking about students?
3. What are the ways that teachers can scaffold the process of student ownership of their learning?
4. How can teachers help students monitor their own learning and set goals for improvement?
5. What are the challenges that teachers face when trying to get students to take ownership of their own learning?

After completing this chapter, revisit these questions and review some final commentary from the authors. See the section Post-Reading Questions near the end of the chapter.

## INTRODUCTION

This chapter begins a new phase of the book. The focus turns to solutions. While it is interesting to contemplate the complexities of past and present assessment practices, all of that thinking and discourse doesn't move a teacher forward in the day-to-day challenges of the classroom. This chapter is designed to help educators examine some of the foundational elements that are needed to move students toward assessment ownership. In addition, it's an opportunity for teachers to reflect on the core beliefs and practices that are needed for this type of assessment culture.

All educators need to be reflective. It is a skill that allows them to be introspective and examine not only their effectiveness but also their level of satisfaction with their work. This chapter is designed to inspire reflective thinking about core beliefs, classroom culture, and, more importantly, ways to get students to take ownership of the learning and assessment cycle.

### A Teacher's Core Beliefs

The famous Brazilian novelist Paulo Coelho has said, "You are what you believe yourself to be." Having a self-identity is an important element in any role that you play. This is especially true for the teaching profession. Teachers need to realize their personal core beliefs and examine how they define themselves and their role in the classroom. In fact, most educators have created a personal philosophy regarding teaching and learning at some stage of their education or practice.

In workshops with teachers, the authors have raised the issue about identifying a teacher's core beliefs. One of the questions posed to teachers is, "Do you believe that *all* students in your class can grow in their learning?" Occasionally, teachers will try to qualify the statement by pointing out students far below grade level as unmotivated or lazy. Sometimes, they are not 100% sure that they believe these struggling students can learn their course content.

Before a teacher or school can transition the classroom to become a place of student-driven decision-making, certain beliefs must be established. Teachers must identify their own philosophies and pedagogical beliefs and agree that, despite a multitude of factors, every student has a desire to learn. Regardless of sociocultural experiences, behaviors, or academic levels, students need opportunities to achieve their personal best.

In addition, the educator must also believe that each student comes to them with perceptions, preconceived notions, and a unique and valuable way in which they view the world. The best thing that an educator can do is to understand what conceptions students have by investing time in conversing with and listening to them. Until the teacher knows what his or her students believe, the educator can't be an advocate for those students and build a classroom culture conducive to their needs.

## Classroom Culture

Before proceeding, it seems appropriate to talk about the term *classroom culture*, since it seems to have multiple interpretations. Teachers must be aware of the multitude of factors that influence classroom culture, which will be explored in detail throughout this chapter. This is important because many aspects of classroom culture directly affect the way teachers and students view classroom assessment.

In searching for the most clear and comprehensive definition of classroom culture, there is one by Mark Windschitl (1999) that seems to most accurately reflect this complex notion. He defines classroom culture as

> a set of beliefs, norms and practices that constitute the fabric of school life. This culture, like all other cultures, affects the way learners can interact with peers, relate to the teacher, and experience the subject matter. The children's relationships with teachers, their patterns of communication, how they are assessed, and even their notion of "what learning is good for" must all be connected, or the culture risks becoming a fragmented collection of practices that fail to reinforce one another. (p. 752)

After reading this definition, you may be overwhelmed and wonder how a teacher could possibly create such a scenario. To be clear, no one has ever said that impassioned and effective teaching was easy. It also is a craft that is honed over time with lots of opportunities for mistakes, learning, and unlearning until teachers find the best ways to connect with their particular student population.

## Asset versus Deficit Thinking

Unfortunately, something that can underpin your classroom culture is *deficit theorizing* (Shields, Bishop, & Mazawi, 2005), a way of thinking about and focusing on students' lack of, or missing, abilities, instead of what skills and talents they add to the classroom environment. This preoccupation with students' deficiencies operates to significantly alter, if not completely incapacitate, affirming and quality teaching practices and behaviors.

Teachers may look at students and see, for example, that they might be lacking English-speaking skills or even basic background knowledge. In some cases, these characteristics are not just viewed as challenges, but are also viewed as deficits. These teaching behaviors not only serve to reinforce negative stereotypes about minority or economically disadvantaged groups, but also affect the teacher's *expectations* of what students can accomplish. In turn, changes in teachers' expectations affect the types of tasks and instructional strategies employed within the classroom.

The following is an example of deficit thinking about economically disadvantaged groups:

> Low income students of all races have . . . a deficit particularly with regard to parental involvement in their education . . . whether assumed to be too busy working, too uneducated to help with homework, or too irresponsible to supervise, low-income parents are commonly considered unable or unwilling to support their children's learning. (Tobin, 2010, p. 3)

The preceding statement not only negatively assumes trends and behaviors about parents before a teacher has actually worked with parents within this community but also serves as a prejudgment that may alter the course of the instructional year. Teachers working with students in challenging situations may adjust their behaviors and, in so doing, reinforce negative stereotypes with one of the following responses to students' needs:

- Alter the content or rigor of classwork, dialogue, and experiences in an effort to meet students at *their* level (i.e., where an individualized education plan, English-language learner modification plan, or other accommodation plan does not exist).
- Avoid assigning home-based tasks or class projects in an effort to accommodate students' home and financial challenges.
- Fail to adequately communicate standards, expectations, or promotion criteria, and the like, for fear that students' parents will not comprehend or be able to support their children in these areas.
- Alter students' grades to higher scores out of fear that stakeholders will hold the teacher accountable for failing to differentiate effectively, or alter students' grades to lower scores out of fear that students may not receive additional services that they may need (e.g., if the student has passing grades but requires additional support, the student may not receive the additional help if his or her grades reflect passing scores).
- Transmit deficit narratives via informal conversations with others—especially those new to the profession, who will, in turn, perpetuate these narratives in thought and through their own professional practices (Pollack, 2012).

Each of these responses, while seemingly altruistic, are actually means by which a teacher can focus on student deficits and widen the chasm between the *haves* and the *have nots*. Moreover, these responses operate to significantly impair, if not completely immobilize, a teacher's sense of professional efficacy—as well as impair the belief that he or she does indeed have the greatest effect on students' social, emotional, and academic development and success.

Interestingly, the previous deficit assumption has a similar effect on the student who experiences academic or social difficulties within affluent communities. Teachers often analyze data by ethnic and socioeconomic subgroups. Consider the following deficit narrative for low-income students: "White, [Asian], and those from affluent backgrounds score higher, on average, than their peers from lower-income backgrounds and their peers of color" (Tobin, 2010, p.1).

Although accounts like this are often touted within nationally comparative reports and lamented throughout political debates, it is important that teachers in either environment understand that an expectation of performance is implied for both groups of students. As previously described, there is the belief that students of color or students residing in lower-income communities will not score as well as their white or more affluent peers.

There is also, however, an assumption that white, Asian, and other affluent groups of students will *and should* score above their peers of color or lower-income backgrounds. The threat inherent within the previous statement is that one's race or affluence predisposes them to academic achievement or that they are more deserving of enrichment experiences.

But what happens to students who are white or Asian or from affluent backgrounds who do not meet this assumption? Do they receive the type of affirming support and in-class interventions that they need in order to succeed, or are they relegated to receive maladaptive teacher responses, or recommended for placement into special education at higher rates merely due to the fact that they learn differently?

What needs to happen is for the team of teachers to move beyond their customary ideals of what constitutes teaching (e.g., collaborative lesson planning, professional development, staff meetings, and parent conferences) to a place of humanistic advocacy that enables teachers to view deficiencies as assets (e.g., what strengths do I see in each student?).

Moreover, teachers must be able to find to a place of resolve that enables them to embrace their flaws through authentic dialogue and investment in their students—to see their students as valuable, accomplished, and willing learners who need their teachers to model humanism, compassion, acceptance, courage, and high expectations. If students do not believe that their teachers are flawed but caring, honest, affirming individuals, then their teachers will not be able to facilitate authentic, student-driven conversations in which their students can feel safe enough to expose and discuss their strengths and weaknesses with them or their peers. The next sections provides an example of an authentic classroom conversation.

## SETTING THE STAGE: DR. BRYSON'S ADVOCACY NARRATIVE
## FOR STUDENTS IN HER PRIMARY CLASSROOM

At the beginning of each academic year, generally within the first two weeks, I hold a preliminary data discussion with my students. Whether facilitating the discussion with first graders or fifth graders, I begin each year by asking my students, "How many of you want to be better readers, mathematicians, social scientists, etc.?" Of course, all hands are raised proudly in the air.

I generally follow this question with a declarative statement, said in an excited whisper, "Awesome! The great thing about my job is that helping you meet your goals is all that I am supposed to—and *want* to—do. But, in order for you to be better at reading or math or science, you must first know *what* it is that you have to learn!"

Without using superfluous or aggrandized language, I use this unique opportunity to provide my students with their grade-level standards and other relevant information pertaining to grade-level promotion. For my first graders, it may sound something like, "In order to head to second grade, you must (1) be able to read at $X$ level, (2) be able to write a complete story, and (3) be able to add and subtract using all types of different strategies."

For my fifth graders, describing to students their promotion criteria may sound something like this: "How many of you *do not* want to be able to understand information that people—especially teachers—may show you in sixth grade? For example, how many of you do not want to be able to read grade-level passages, solve math problems, or would simply prefer to stay in elementary school instead of going on to middle school next year?"

Of course, no hands go up—unless they did not understand the reversed-nature of the question or were trying to engender a response. To either of the reasons, I would repeat the question by phrasing it in such a way that there is no confusion: "I want to make sure that I understand you. You would rather have trouble reading, solving math problems, or stay in fifth grade instead of go on to middle school next year?" It is then that the student either self-corrects his or her misconception or adamantly agrees that she or he would prefer to stay in the current grade.

If the student simply misunderstood, I proceed with a whole-group conversation in which I tell them my role and responsibility as their teacher and we discuss as a class what is required (e.g., standardized assessment, in-class assignments and assessments, grading rules, and the like). However, if the student insists on holding the position that staying behind is preferable to moving forward, remembering my philosophy about students wanting to achieve their personal best, I would ask, "Why do you prefer to stay behind?"

It is then that I am often informed of some of the student's long-standing fears (i.e., academic, social, and/or emotional), as well as begin to understand the value that education has for that student. This type of empathetic communication conveys my authentic investment in the well-being and success of all of my students. The way in which I reflectively listen and respond to their ambitions and concerns assures all students that I am committed to supporting their growth.

It is important that I, as well as other teachers, understand that until students know that you are personally invested in their success—whatever that success may be (i.e., academic, social, or behavior-oriented)—everything that you do in your classroom has little actual bearing or personal relevance for them. Students must know that you are personally invested in them in order for you to serve as a respected advocate to help them to achieve *their* personal best.

## Analyzing the Data

During this segment of the process of teaching students to own their data, I show students, either as a whole group or during a one-on-one conference, their assessment data and explain to students how they obtained these scores. In my particular district, we employ a benchmark, or quarterly assessment system.

In addition to formative assessments in reading, writing, and mathematics, we also employ the use of a standardized assessment that all students across the district take. In terms of the reading assessment, I review students' reading running records following the conclusion of their one-on-one reading assessment, or review our class's averages as well as each student's score.

I dialogue with the students about their strengths and my sense of pride for the skills that they have mastered. However, I also dialogue with students about things that I have noticed during the reading session or noticed in the score report that they should be aware of going forward (e.g., decoding behaviors, omissions, fluency rate, or even comprehension). Although many teachers are fearful that students will feel self-conscious and will therefore take on a negative affect toward reading and assessment, this is the *exact opposite* of what I have experienced as a classroom teacher.

Students who become aware of their strengths accept praise and become empowered to improve. They *want* to advance to the next level of mastery. They often pair themselves with those students who have mastered the skill they are trying to learn, and because of this awareness that we all face different challenges, they are increasingly more willing to help others who want to master what they are good at doing.

The data dialogue merely provides an opportunity to show that as a class, we all make mistakes and we can work together to minimize them. For example, I have often had students come up to me, saying, "I really did not know how to read this book using conversation language, but now I can because my friend helped me read it the way that we talk!"

If I keep my knowledge of my students' challenges to myself, then this will make *me* the person who is *solely* responsible for whether or not those challenges are met. However, if I share my observations with the students who need the guidance, then I increase the likelihood that they will know what their areas of strength and challenge are and they can work toward independently noticing and monitoring those areas.

Remember, the purpose of teaching and learning is to honor our roles as educators, which is to cultivate better readers, writers, mathematicians, scientists, and creators by believing in and creating an environment that affirms their abilities and interests.

**One student's perspective.** Over my years as a teacher and full-time graduate student, I was responsible for conducting numerous interviews for some of my qualitative research projects. One such project granted me a unique opportunity to informally interview one of my students who had made some impressive improvements in mathematics class. The interview provided me a remarkable opportunity to see the effectiveness of my classroom practices. Although the full interview is available on the book's companion website, it is important that I communicate the overarching themes that I gleaned from the interview, which included:

1. The supportive classroom environment matters.
2. Communicating progress informs and motivates students' performance.
3. Given the opportunity, students will communicate instructional changes that would better facilitate their learning.

Again, the role and responsibility of the teacher is to provide an environment that allows for and promotes student learning and teacher development. This does not mean handing over classroom management and instructional practices to the students; after all, you are the trained educator in the classroom. However, it does mean giving students an opportunity to weigh in on classroom protocols and procedures in a meaningful way to not only affect students' behavior and performance, but also to honor their voice and perspectives.

## STUDENT OWNERSHIP IN ACTION: A PERSONAL VIGNETTE OF ACTUAL CLASSROOM PRACTICE

The concept of student ownership of data can be a difficult concept to visualize—harder still, to operationalize. How can educators meaningfully teach students, especially younger students, to understand how to make their data function as the precursor to their self-selected, intentional learning? Not only is it possible to foster an environment conducive to student-owned data, but also it is viable within the classroom, as described in the previous section, which is based on one of the author's personal teaching experiences.

**Data dialogues.** If a team of teachers (or local school) wishes to begin data dialogues within the classroom, you may consider providing students with their actual tests (if possible) or score reports.

*Note:* Please follow the state and district's confidentiality rules regarding the sharing of assessments and assessment data with students. If conflicting information exists regarding permissible sharing, err on the side of caution. Speak with the grade-level administrator, principal, area superintendent, or district assessment office when in doubt.

Conduct an *Item Error Analysis* as a whole group, small group, or with individual students. The exact size of the discussion group will depend on the purpose of the assessment or data dialogue. If the purpose is to understand why the class's proficiency average is at a certain level, then a whole group discussion may be appropriate. However, if the purpose is to help a specific student notice a pattern of errors, then an individual conference may be more responsive to meet a student's needs.

Regardless, this analysis of errors is the most revealing in terms of knowing and understanding the students' line of reasoning and their unique perspectives and interpretations of the assessment as it not only encourages a dialogue about why students may have selected a particular distractor option versus the correct answer, but also permits the students to understand the structure and content of the assessment.

Allow students with correct responses to assessment items to articulate their reasoning behind their selection. This step not only helps the class hear a different perspective, but also allows students who may not have scored so well on the entirety of the assessment to have a voice within the data dialogue as well.

Dialogue with the students about how each of the test items—especially those that were missed—relate to the long-term objective of demonstrating content mastery and promotion standards to enter the next grade.

**Creating individualized student goal plans.** Following a data dialogue, work with students to create individualized education plans. These are different from the individualized education plans (IEPs) that are customized for students identified with disabilities. However, contrary to popular belief and use, designing goal plans should not be limited to students being served through special education. A suggested name for this learning growth plan is *My Individual Plan and Goals* (MIPAG). Teachers can work with students to customize a MIPAG and set goals tailored specifically to their learning needs.

A possible route to employing the MIPAG and goal-setting process could be via the following:

1. Students obtain, or have at least viewed, an individual report of their strengths and weaknesses per content area.
2. Whether in first or fifth grade, students take time to read the report and understand their strengths and challenges, as well as how close they are to mastering the grade-level objectives for that content area. For example, in reading, first graders could receive their running record with strengths indicated with smiley faces and challenges noted via highlighting. Fifth graders may receive a disaggregated reading report that shows the subdomains that they have mastered as well as the subdomains that they need to work on improving. Students in grades 6–12 may benefit from finding other authentic ways in which to record their data—be it a chart with standards, or via establishing and writing intermediate, content-specific goals related to the overarching objective of the course or class.
3. Students read the report, decide on the skill or domain that they need to improve, and then set a goal via a list of actions to achieve proficiency on the self-selected skill for the next few weeks or quarter.
4. Students record their data, observations, and goals for the next benchmark assessment in a notebook or portfolio, which they will use to monitor interim progress before the next benchmark assessment (see table 3.1 and figures 3.1 and 3.2).

**Guiding students through meaningful instructional decisions.** Once students have recorded their data and observations as well as articulated new goals to achieve before the next data dialogue, it is time for the teacher to demonstrate expertise via the experiential art of *teaching*. It is at this crucial juncture that the teacher suggests and provides meaningful activities that would help students better understand and master the subdomains that they have set as improvement goals.

This is the segment within the process where the teacher relates how the literature circle center/rotation that occurs during reading workshop will aid in developing their narrative language or inference skills, or in increasing their previous reading level, as well as express how using math journals (in any grade level) will help them conceptualize and master operations with addition and subtraction, fractions, algebra, or statistics.

The beauty of this part of the cycle is that students are incredibly invested in their learning. They understand that every instructional decision that the teacher makes, as well as any activities that the teacher has selected to employ—either within the classroom as a whole group, small group, or with an individual student—is done with the intention to help each of them meet the short-term goals described within their self-directed MIPAG and their long-term goal of moving on to the next grade.

**Table 3.1. Reading-Level Data (star indicates the range where student should be performing)**

| | | | |
|---|---|---|---|
| Z | Z | Z | Z★ |
| Y | Y | Y | Y★ |
| X | X | X | X★ |
| W | W | W★ | W★ |
| V | V★ | V★ | V★ |
| U★ | U★ | U★ | U★ |
| T★ | T★ | T | T |
| S★ | S | S | S |
| R | R | R | R |
| Q | Q | Q | Q |
| P | P | P | P |
| O | O | O | O |
| N | N | N | N |
| M | M | M | M |
| L | L | L | L |
| K | K | K | K |
| J | J | J | J |
| I | I | I | I |
| H | H | H | H |
| G | G | G | G |
| F | F | F | F |
| E | E | E | E |
| D | D | D | D |
| C | C | C | C |
| B | B | B | B |
| A | A | A | A |
| Baseline | Fall | Winter | Spring |

Note: At the beginning of the year, the teacher assesses the students' reading levels. The students then record their levels (as a bar graph) as they change throughout the year.

The challenge of having students understand the value of the assignments/tasks that the teacher selects has been removed because students (a) trust their teacher's expertise and intentions and (b) are willing and motivated to employ that trust to improve their content area background and proficiency.

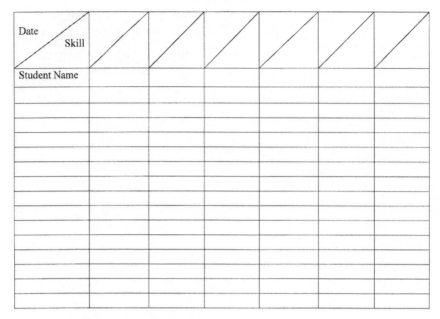

| Date \ Skill  Student Name | | | | | | |
|---|---|---|---|---|---|---|
| | | | | | | |
| | | | | | | |
| | | | | | | |
| | | | | | | |
| | | | | | | |
| | | | | | | |
| | | | | | | |
| | | | | | | |
| | | | | | | |
| | | | | | | |
| | | | | | | |
| | | | | | | |
| | | | | | | |
| | | | | | | |

**Figure 3.1.    Literature circle novel data.**

Dear _____,

At the beginning of the school year, I was reading on a level _____.

Now I am reading on a level _____.

The next time we talk, I would like to be reading on a level _____.

I will do these things to help me meet my reading goal:

(1) _____

_____.

(2) _____

_____

_____.

Thank you for helping me reach my reading goals!

Signed,

_____

**Figure 3.2.    Second-grade student goals sheet.**

*A word of caution!* The only thing that classroom teachers have to remember is that *consistency is key*. The teacher cannot begin dialoguing, recording, and developing goals for students' progress without maintenance. Maintenance requires monitoring and cycling back, both of which will be discussed shortly.

If, at any point, teachers realize that this task is more than they can handle (which is understandable because teachers must first understand and be able to manage the dynamics of classroom management before accommodating student-driven ownership), they should not merely end the process without honoring the work that the students have done and without formally concluding the data dialogues. Without this closure, students will feel that their teachers have been haphazard about their goals and that the intention to honor their progress and goals was not genuine.

**Monitoring students' progress.** The next segment of the student-ownership cycle is to monitor how students progress through the meaningful tasks that they have been assigned. This is the point in time in which the teacher— serving as the classroom guide and facilitator—must check students' understandings via informative assessments and summative activities (see chapter 4), or some other authentic assessment, and refine instructional choices to continue to engage and inspire students to meet their goals.

If something is not working, dialogue with students about why they think it is not working. Ask them for their perspective regarding their progress and allow them to communicate what roadblocks are impeding their progress.

Remember to be open to and honor their perspectives and opinions. Please do not take it personally if little Sarah says that working with the group is driving her crazy. Despite what teachers may know and believe about cooperative and homogenous grouping of students, if a student communicates an impediment to progress, remove it so that the student's request can be honored and the opportunity for learning can be optimized. Opportunities for cooperative and homogenous grouping can occur during a different activity or can be slowly integrated within the current instructional segment.

Moreover, if things are working (in terms of classroom management) and progress is being made, no matter how seemingly insignificant, *communicate* these successes so that students are aware that progress is being made and so that the students can articulate to current (and subsequent) faculty what conditions best prime them for learning and for achieving their personal best.

**Cycling back.** Finally, whenever new data become available, formatively or summatively, informal or standardized, the teacher's responsibility as a data guide and facilitator is to revisit the students' progress via repeating the student data ownership process, being sure to adjust the students' activities to further support or master new objectives and goals.

This is the essence of *learning* and *teaching*. Teachers and students must decide, based on the academic standards and/or goals, what teaching needs to occur to foster growth and facilitate mastery. *Never forget to cycle back to the data in order to guide students in understanding their strengths and challenges.*

## THE BEST OF BOTH WORLDS

No one can refute the inherent benefits of both formative and summative assessments. Summative assessments operate to guide incremental instructional decisions, which are *formatively* assessed during poignant or benchmark segments of the instructional cycle. The question is: How do we meaningfully create and use these assessments with the objectives of both (a) improving instructional praxis and (b) improving students' awareness of their own learning, while keeping in mind the roots and traditional roles of assessment?

The authors believe that one means by which to bridge the chasm between the traditional roles of assessment and the contemporary needs and utilities of assessments is student self-assessment via self-regulation. These topics will be discussed in chapter 5.

## POST-READING QUESTIONS

The questions are first listed for readers to contemplate on their own. Additionally, the questions are listed a second time with commentary from the authors' perspective.

1. How would you describe classroom culture?
2. What are examples of teachers having asset versus deficit thinking about students?
3. What are the ways that teachers can scaffold the process of student ownership of their learning?
4. How can teachers help students monitor their own learning and set goals for improvement?
5. What are the challenges that teachers face when trying to get students to take ownership of their own learning?

## POST-READING QUESTIONS

**How would you describe classroom culture?** When you hear teachers talk about classroom culture, numerous mental images might come to mind. Some might think about the behavioral management style or the teacher's disposition. Others might hone in on the word *culture* and think about the way that teachers understand and respect students of all socioeconomic backgrounds and abilities. Then again, some might focus on teachers' instructional philosophy and their beliefs about the role of teachers and students in the learning environment.

In this chapter, we offered a comprehensive definition of *classroom culture*. So in essence, we are talking about all of these elements, and that's what makes the topic so complex. Classroom culture is an enormous part of the whole assessment equation because it impacts the way that assessment is framed in the mind of the teacher and the students. Improving classroom climate is a constant reflective process for teachers.

In our opinion, based in part on Anaya's specific research (Bryson, 2016) on teacher reflection, teachers are not given enough time to reflect about the type of classroom culture they establish. One suggestion that we would make that has helped us both to self-analyze our own teaching and improve our classroom culture is reading literature on teacher reflection. Here's some recommended reading:

> *Reflective Practice for Teachers* by Maura Sellars (Especially helpful for novice or pre-service teachers.)
> *Promoting Reflective Thinking in Teachers: 50 Action Strategies* by Germaine L. Taggart and Alfred P. Wilson (Helpful and practical reflective techniques for all classroom teachers.)
> *The Critically Reflective Teacher* by Stephen D. Brookfield (This book is our mutual favorite. It is written for higher education faculty but we have found very useful for P–12 teachers as well.)

**What are examples of teachers having asset versus deficit thinking about students?** The concept of deficit thinking first came across our radar screen when reading an article by Lois Weiner (2006) entitled, "Challenging Deficit Thinking." Since both of us have had experiences working in urban communities with challenging and high-stakes assessment demands, we could relate to teacher talk about student deficits. Weiner asserts that teachers need to "acknowledge deficit explanations and examine them critically. Invariably, this illuminates possibilities that have eluded us, including strategies that focus on student strengths" (p. 44).

In the context of this book's focus on loving assessment, the idea about focusing on student assets first is essential. Yes, there are deficits, and we need to work on improving these areas of weakness. However, we can't move students forward without an "asset-first" approach to teaching and learning. One key way to fully embrace assessment is to love the way it can empower students' awareness about their own strengths and specific areas where they can improve.

**What are the ways that teachers can scaffold the process of student ownership of their learning?** In our humble opinion, student ownership of learning and assessment is not an option. It is an essential requirement to embracing and enjoying the assessment process. That being said, the process of implementing and scaffolding this process is complex. The example of the steps that Anaya has been using in her classroom shows how a teacher can operationalize the process.

For more specific details and an in-depth explanation of the student ownership process, we recommend the book *Partnering with Students: Building Ownership of Learning* by Mary Jane O'Connell and Kara Vandas.

**How can teachers help students monitor their own learning and set goals for improvement?** Hopefully, the examples and suggestions in this chapter have shown that students can be taught to monitor their own learning when their own assessment data are given and explained and they are provided the opportunity to consider feasible goals for them to move forward. Students want to know how they can advance to their goal, whether it is reaching the next grade level, graduating high school, and/or pursuing a career or higher education. We believe, along with Ryan and Deci (see more on these authors' theory in chapter 5), that all human beings have an innate desire for autonomy and competence.

In a recent visit to an Atlanta school that was once deemed a "failing" institution, we spoke with the principal about how she was able to turn the school around. Her overwhelming sense was that the school's improvement was caused by the increased emphasis on students taking ownership of their own learning and growth.

You can't make a student learn. There has to be some personal ownership of the learning process. When students understand that assessment is a tool to gauge their learning, not a tool to rebuke or punish them, then forward thinking can prevail.

Here's a good analogy for you. Think about a superhighway with cars speeding along four lanes during rush hour. Everyone is making moves, passing slow drivers, and maneuvering around curves and exits. However, there are safety precautions in place like speed limits, median barriers, and guardrails. As a driver, you have to take ownership of your own safety by following strategies like buckling your seat belt, refraining from texting, and staying within the speed limit. All of these personal decisions help you reach your destination goal safely.

Similarly, students need to be shown that there are specific precautions in place for them to succeed, like sequenced course content, teacher support, and peer collaboration. However, they must assume ownership by taking some personal responsibility. They must put in effort, seek help when struggling, and take advantage of available resources. As teachers, you can help make students aware of the benefits they receive when they take ownership of their learning.

**What are the challenges that teachers face when trying to get students to take ownership of their own learning?** We are not here to tell you that the process of a positive classroom culture that promotes student owner-ship of learning is easy. It is, indeed, quite the contrary. The challenges are many, including the classic problems of time, support, and most of all the knowledge and skills to know how to implement the process.

Of course, there are the usual solutions like coaching, professional learn-ing, and background reading and research on ways to begin a strategic pro-cess of student-data dialogues and goal setting. The biggest challenge that we have seen is that there are teachers who are in settings where they are not getting the needed support to conduct these types of assessment strategies.

If you are a teacher who does not feel supported to promote student ownership of learning and assessment, there are some ways that you can effectively advocate for the use of these techniques.

1. *Do your homework and be informed.* The first step in advocating for change is to be highly informed about your topic. You can't make your case if you don't have the background knowledge and data to prove your point. Read everything you can about the topic. Search online to join blogs or twitter feeds about the issue. Make sure you thoroughly understand the problem and have some concrete solutions in mind.

2. *Find out baseline knowledge and work on getting buy-in.* Explore the level of understanding that currently exists about student ownership of learning. Talk to your administrators, peers, students, and parents to see what they already know and how they feel about the topic. This inquiry phase also helps to build buy-in.

3. *Frame your message about improvement—not about judgment.* As with any educational advocacy technique, you always want to ap-proach others, especially those in power, with a positive message about how these techniques, first of all, benefit students. There are numerous research studies that have been conducted to demonstrate the benefits of student ownership and formative assessment to raise student achievement. For example, see this research study, "Promot-ing Student Ownership of Learning through High-Impact Formative Assessment Practices," available at https://www.researchgate.net/publication/40423915_Promoting_Student_Ownership_of_Learning_Through_High-Impact_Formative_Assessment_Practices.

In addition, this book's companion website has updated links regarding this topic.

# REFERENCES

Brookfield, S. D. (2017). *Becoming a critically reflective teacher* (2nd ed.). San Francisco, CA: Jossey-Bass.

Bryson, A. L. (2016). *The effects of critical reflection on the development of novice, elementary mathematics teachers' perceived efficacy.* (Doctoral dissertation). Retrieved from Mercer University Libraries Catalog. Call No. LB2386 .B797 2016.

O'Connell, M. J., & Vandas, K. L. (2015). *Partnering with students: Building ownership of learning.* Thousand Oaks, CA: Corwin Press.

Pollack, T. M. (2012). The miseducation of a beginning teacher: One educator's critical reflection on the functions and power of deficit narratives. *Multicultural Perspectives, 14*(2), 93–98. doi: 10.1080/15210960.2012.673318

Sellars, M. (2014). *Reflective practice for teachers.* Los Angeles: Sage.

Shields, C., Bishop, R., & Mazawi, A. (2005). *Pathologizing practices: The impact of deficit thinking on education.* New York, NY: Peter Lang.

Taggart, G. L., & Wilson, A. P. (2005). *Promoting reflective thinking in teachers: 50 action strategies.* Thousand Oaks, CA: Corwin Press.

Tobin, K. J., (2010, August). *The Persistence and role of deficit thinking in new teachers' perceptions of students' backgrounds.* Paper presented at the annual meeting of the American Sociological Association Annual Meeting, Hilton Atlanta and Atlanta Marriott Marquis, Atlanta, GA. Retrieved from http://citation.allacademic.com/meta/p410352_index.html

Weiner, L. (2006). Challenging deficit thinking. *Educational Leadership, 64*(1), 42–45.

Windschitl, M. (1999). The challenges of sustaining a constructivist classroom culture. *Phi Delta Kappan, 80*(10), 751–755.

*Chapter Four*

# Solution Two

*Focus on Instructive Assessment*

"When a teacher teaches, no matter how well he or she might design a lesson, what a child learns is unpredictable. Children do not always learn what we teach. That is why the most important assessment does not happen at the end of learning—it happens during the learning, when there is still time to do something with the information."—Dylan Wiliam

## PRE-READING QUESTIONS

Before reading this chapter, consider your prior knowledge/opinions regarding these questions:

1. What comes to mind when you hear the term *instructive assessment*?
2. How would you describe the benefits of formative assessments to students . . . to teachers?
3. How would formative assessments vary based on the stage of learning?
4. Should formative assessments be graded?
5. How are you increasing your use of formative assessment techniques?

After completing this chapter, revisit these questions and review some final commentary from the authors. See the section Post-Reading Questions near the end of the chapter.

## INTRODUCTION

The term *assessment* invokes a vast array of images in the minds of stake-holders, teachers, and students. In a recent workshop on assessment, a large group of teachers was asked this question: "What's the first word that comes to mind when you hear the term 'assessment'?" The group responded with words like "tests," "accountability," "grades," and even the word "anxiety." It seems that most educators tend to bundle assessment into its summative uses—the evaluation that happens after learning has historically taken the front seat. This is unfortunate because the most powerful assessments for learners and teachers are formative assessments.

### Evaluative versus Instructive Assessment

Assessment that is focused on instruction has more positive connotations than assessment for evaluation. Although it may sound novel, the concept of instructive assessment is not new. Terms used to describe instructive assessment include formative assessment, informative assessment, assessment *for* learning, and in-process evaluation.

When these terms are unpacked, they all lead to the same question: How is instruction being evaluated and modified based on the level of student understanding during the stages of learning? A better approach is one that occurs throughout a lesson when teachers pose questions such as: "Are students understanding? Do they get it? What are the misconceptions?"

Instructive assessment that is effective and strategic puts a laser-like focus on what learners are grasping and how they can articulate that learning. In the early acquisition stages of learning a new concept, an adept teacher will stop and check for understanding every few minutes. Strategic questions will be raised such as, "Who can explain in their own words what was just taught?" Or better yet, each student will have a few minutes to explain to a partner the essence of that chunk of the lesson.

During this type of activity, the teacher should walk around and listen intently to student explanations to see if there are any misunderstandings. If the goal is for understanding, then the students are the barometers of this understanding and constant clarifications are necessary to make sure that accurate content is being absorbed.

### Benefits of Instructive Assessment

Instructive assessments, unlike summative assessments, allow students and teachers to gather more detailed understandings of student abilities and can be used to guide remediation, re-teaching, and selecting instructional strategies. Numerous scholars and extensive research studies have documented the long-term benefits to student achievement from the use of formative assessment (Black & Wiliam, 1998; Marzano & Brown, 2009; Stiggins, Arter, Chappuis, & Chappuis, 2006).

**Benefits to teachers.** Instructive assessment provides immediate information to teachers regarding student knowledge levels. The use of well-timed feedback from students enables teachers to quickly adjust instruction while learning is in progress. It says to the teacher, "Here's what students know" or "Here's where they are confused."

**Benefits to students.** Informative assessment helps students in several ways. It allows opportunities for students to be owners of their learning and to self-assess. Students can see if they understand or if they need clarification. It also allows for quick breaks in the learning. Students need mental breaks to help solidify and clarify what they have heard, seen, or read. Students are actively engaged in the learning process when they are participating in formative assessments. Furthermore, students benefit from adjustments that the teacher makes to improve instruction.

## What about Grading Instructive Assessment?

A common question that pops up in conversations about instructive assessment is the issue of grading. Teachers have valid concerns about the ways to quantify instructional progress. Some schools require a certain number of recorded grades per marking period. However, this does not validate a drive for grading formative assessments. There should be ample informal and formal summative assessments to fill a grade book.

More importantly, the focus must remain on giving students specific feedback during instruction so that they can correct mistakes and grow in their understandings. This feedback needs to be viewed by the students as non-evaluative and purely instructive. When students receive this kind of feedback, it is showing them that the assessment is for their benefit and not a form of "gotcha" mentality.

There are several ways that teachers can track progress during instructive assessments. Of course, the age-old technique of observation is one of the most powerful tools for teachers. Teachers who are carefully watching, listening, and tuning in to student responses can automatically make instructional corrections on the fly. A savvy teacher is like a hawk, eyeing every opportunity to swoop in and clarify a misconception.

Additional strategies for recording progress include keeping anecdotal records and checklists. Teachers might have a checklist of student names and learning targets and record the stage of progress. For example, a checklist such as the one in figure 4.1 could be used to indicate the skill, date of the assessment, and the formative progress.

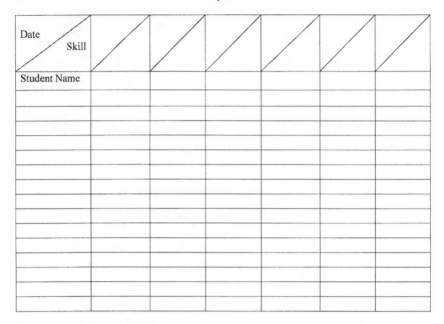

**Figure 4.1.  Skills checklist.**

Some teachers have students keep skill checklists in their agenda books so that students can track their own progress. This strategy is a useful way to have students take ownership of their learning processes and visually track their own growth. There are also effective electronic tools for tracking progress, including spreadsheets and Google docs. (See more resources on the book's companion website.) The main concern is that students receive some specific feedback and that they take action to move forward in their learning based on this feedback.

## Specific Feedback

In an issue of *The Economist*, dated June 11, 2016, the cover theme was emblazoned with the catchy phrase "How to Make a Good Teacher." The concept that great teaching can be taught was prevalent throughout the theme articles. One startling statistic that was cited from the Education Endowment Foundation (2016) stated that "feedback to pupils" has the highest effectiveness rating in raising student achievement. Moreover, it was emphasized that the skill of giving effective feedback can and should be explicitly taught to teachers.

All teachers and students are familiar with feedback. Instructors frequently tell learners: "good job," "well done," "way to go," or "try again." However, these generic phrases do little to help students know specifically what they did well and what they need to improve. Therefore, the art of giving specific feedback is worthy of being honed.

Imagine the scenario where a student submits a draft of a writing assignment and a teacher responds with the phrase "Good start; keep working." In contrast, consider the teacher reply "Your use of adjectives is strong, but you need to work on your run-on sentences." The first feedback statement is vague and gives no specific direction. Students need to be given specific feedback about their strengths and areas for growth, be held accountable, and be provided with support and time to make needed changes.

One of the most helpful resources for teachers to learn the art of feedback is a book entitled *How to Give Effective Feedback to Your Students* by Susan M. Brookhart. This text includes suggestions for oral, written, and content-specific feedback. Brookhart (2008) writes,

> Feedback says to a student, "Somebody cared enough about my work to read it and think about it!" Most teachers want to be that "somebody." Feedback matches specific descriptions and suggestions with a particular student's work. It is just-in-time, just-for-me information delivered when and where it can do the most good. (p. 1)

A promising sign is that this task of giving specific feedback to each individual student is being reiterated in pre-service education. For example, a national teacher certification assessment, edTPA (Teacher Performance Assessment, http://edtpa.aacte.org/) has a requirement that teacher candidates submit student work samples that show specific feedback, indicating what the students did well, and specific guidance for skills that need improvement based on the designated learning objectives. The edTPA does not accept vague or generic feedback.

There is clearly a movement in education to understand the strong benefits from effective and specific feedback. As educators become more adept at this skill, more active participation from students will be promoted. Instead of receiving a final test grade, glancing at it, and throwing it away, students must be taught how to act on formative feedback and become accountable for making improvements.

## Adding Variety to Instructive Assessment

Another consideration that is relevant to the discussion of informative assessment is the need for variety. In the coming portions of this chapter, a broad variety of strategies will be presented to assist teachers with implementing ongoing assessments in the classroom. An important concept for teachers to keep in mind is the idea of variety and the strategic use of assessment strategies to match the stages of learning and the needs of the learners.

Eric Jensen, a proponent of applying neuroscience to teaching, explained in his classic book, *Teaching with the Brain in Mind* (1998), that the brain likes variety. Novel strategies can be a brain stimulator, so he encourages teachers to employ an interesting new strategy when there is a lull or when the teacher wants to mentally link the novelty of the strategy to the skill being taught.

Interestingly, the brain also likes ritual. Thus, common familiar tasks also have a role in memory retention. Part of the art and science of being an effective teacher includes finding ways to balance ritual and novelty. Reuse those tried and true effective strategies, and save those novel exciting techniques for a challenging concept.

## IMPLEMENTING INFORMATIVE ASSESSMENT FOR STAGES OF LEARNING

Different strategies may be needed for different stages in the learning process. When a new concept is being presented, teachers need to activate prior knowledge and make sure students have a way to elicit connections to their previous understandings. Teachers should also conduct numerous quick checks for understanding during the acquisition of knowledge to see if students truly understand and identify misconceptions. After learning, the teacher should have a glimpse of how well students understood key elements of the lesson in order to make any needed adjustments for the next lesson.

Each of these stages may have strategies that lend themselves to the learning juncture. Then again, some strategies are so ubiquitous that they can be adapted for any stage of learning. Some crafty experienced teachers might even argue that they can take any strategy and find a way to make it fit their needs for any time or any level.

Keeping these learning stages in mind, this next section of the chapter presents strategies for four broad categories: before learning, during learning, after learning, and anytime learning.

As mentioned previously, a teacher may see a particular strategy as being useful for a different stage than suggested, and that is fine. All of the strategies listed can be modified and adapted to meet different age levels and content areas. The goal is to add as many informative assessment strategies to a teacher's tool kit as possible.

### Before Learning

The concept of checking for prior knowledge is nothing new. Teachers have been trained to use strategies that activate previous learning and know these are important. However, in an environment built on using assessment as a way to inform instruction, prior knowledge checks are not just a step written on a lesson plan, but a strategic way of validating and building on students' background knowledge and making learning relevant to real-life scenarios.

Take for instance the following example of a high school science teacher introducing a new learning segment in chemistry. The teacher might start the initial lesson by having the statement "Properties of Matter" on the board. As students enter the room, she instructs her students to take out their science journals and jot down as many things as they can about the statement in one minute.

While this is not a totally ineffective technique, think about how much more powerful it would be to show a short video of the main properties of matter such as mass, weight, impenetrability, inertia, porosity, form, volume, and density. Next, have the students work in small groups to brainstorm real-life examples for each property. This is personalizing the activation of back-ground knowledge for the students. Finally, students share examples with the class and the teacher helps clarify any misconceptions. This is an example of before-learning assessment in maximum form.

## Before-Learning Strategies

*The Brick Wall or Graffiti Wall*

*Materials: Colored markers, brick wall paper (See 4.1 brick wall handouts on the book's companion website.)*

Small groups of students are given colored markers and one large piece of paper that has a brick wall pattern. (See the brick wall handouts on this book's companion website, as well as suggestions for purchasing butcher block brick paper.) Students brainstorm what they already know about a topic on the wall using graffiti-style writing. One technique that helps the teacher identify individual responses is to have each student use a different colored marker and put their name on the edge of the wall somewhere. After students have a few minutes to brainstorm and record their ideas, stop and take time to share. Go around to each group and have them give one word or phrase from their wall.

The teacher (or a student who is a fast writer) can record these responses on a board/chart. Go around several times, having students give words that have not been said before. Next, it is important for the teacher to clarify that these words indeed match the new topic and point out the prior knowledge they are bringing to the new learning. A copy of each group's brick or graffiti wall might be posted in the classroom.

*What's in Your Head?*

*Materials: Blank paper, writing tools*

Activate thinking with this strategy to elicit background knowledge. Students draw a picture of a large empty head like the one in figure 4.2. Then, students fill the head with all the words and phrases that they can think of related to the day's lesson. Students share and the teacher checks for any misconceptions.

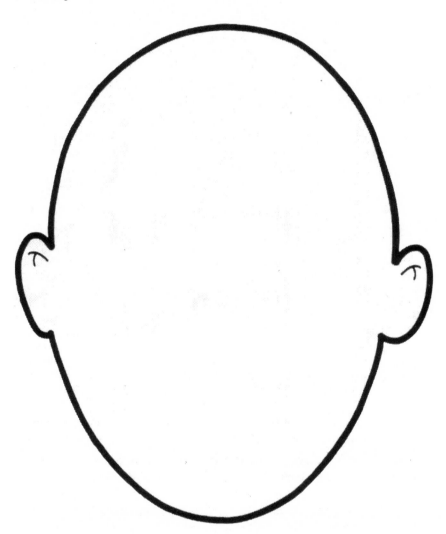

**Figure 4.2. Empty head.**

## Brain Dump

*Materials: Post-it notes, pencils, large paper (See 4.2 brain dump handouts on the book's companion website.)*

Form small groups. First, each person in the group should dump (write out) from their brain all the words or phrases about the topic on a sticky note. Next, each person adds his or her note to the group paper. (See figure 4.3.) Share thoughts that were alike or different. Summarize the group's prior knowledge and share with the class. Alternatively, each student could have a handout and fill in their ideas and then share with the group. Of course, the teacher must validate and clarify any mistaken concepts.

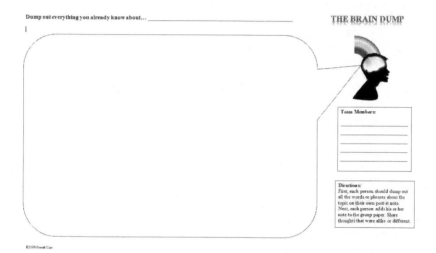

**Figure 4.3. Brain dump.**

## Word Sort and Level of Understanding Board

*Materials: List of key vocabulary words related to new learning segment, scissors, baggies (See 4.3 word sort board on the book's companion website.)*

This strategy is extremely helpful when introducing a new learning segment that has a great deal of key vocabulary. Students can gain confidence over time in understanding the terms, and the teacher can gauge the level of knowledge of the terms at varying stages during the learning unit. Begin by giving the students a list of the key words. Have the students cut these out. Next, give the students a sorting board. (See figure 4.4.)

The board has four columns, indicating various levels of knowledge of the term:

**Word Sort Board**

| I know very well. I can explain to someone else. | I know a little bit. I know some things about it. | I might know it? I'm not really sure. I still need help with this word. | I don't have a clue. |
|---|---|---|---|
| | | | |

**Figure 4.4.   Word sort board.**

1. I know very well and can explain to someone else.
2. I know some things about it.
3. I might know, but I still need some help.
4. I don't have a clue.

After the first sort, have students share the results of their sorts. See if students can help each other, especially if a student knows a word very well and can explain to a peer.

The teacher can monitor the activity and try to gauge what words are the most and least familiar. A neat idea is to take a photo of each student's sorted word board. Have the students store the words in a small baggie to use again. At midpoint and at the end of the learning segment, have students sort the words again and compare their results to prior photos of their sorting boards. This is a good way for students to monitor their own growth in understanding key vocabulary.

## During-Learning Strategies

One of the most powerful and strategic techniques a teacher can employ during the learning of new material is to check for understanding. It seems like everyone would agree that this is an obvious teaching strategy that even the most novice teacher would understand. However, after teaching in and observing numerous classrooms, it is clear that this key technique is not used as often or as strategically as it could be.

Mary Budd Rowe (1986) conducted some interesting research in which she found that the average amount of time a student can absorb new information, especially via teacher talk, is 10 minutes. Yes, that's right! Chunk the delivery of new information into 10-minute bits. After each bit of new information, stop and take a few minutes to have students restate, clarify, illustrate, or just talk about what they just learned. To accomplish this *during learning assessment*, teachers need a bag full of strategies to mix up review approaches.

### Questioning

Questioning is an age-old technique that teachers can easily take for granted. Teachers who are highly effective, however, utilize extensive questioning strategies (see videos of effective teaching on the teachingchannel.org) by asking questions such as "Who can explain the first part of what we just learned?" or "How does what we just learned connect to what we talked about yesterday?"

Using various levels of thinking in questioning is another important element. Teachers can build confidence by starting with easy questions and then building up to questions that have students comparing, analyzing, evaluating, or justifying information from the lesson. There are numerous helpful online tools with question stems aligned to Bloom's Taxonomy (http://www.bloomstaxonomy.org/Blooms%20Taxonomy%20questions.pdf) or Webb's Depth of Knowledge (http://svesd.net/files/DOK_Question_Stems.pdf).

What follows next are some questioning techniques.

### Question Dots

*Materials: Template with question dots handout (see 4.4 question dots handout on the book's companion website), pencils, one die per group*

The teacher or, better yet, the students need to create six open-ended questions about the current lesson topic. Form the class into groups and have each group write the questions on a question dots template. (See figure 4.5.) Students then roll a die to determine which question to ask first. Students take turns responding. If the same number is rolled, encourage the students to

**Sample Question Dots**

Students can use the questions or create new questions in each box.

| Question: | Question: | Question: |
|---|---|---|
| What was an important vocabulary word in this lesson? | What was a part of the lesson that was most difficult to understand? | What was a part of the lesson that was easiest to understand? |
| Question: | Question: | Question: |
| Explain a part of the lesson to the group. Try to use a visual/drawing to explain. | What was a big idea in the lesson? | How does today's lesson connect to something you have learned before? |

**Figure 4.5.   Sample question dots.**

respond to the same question in a different way. Keep rolling the die until all the questions have been covered.

As an alternative accountability element, have students record the number of the question and their response on a piece of paper and turn this in to the teacher for review. This is a quick and easy way for teachers to see the depth of understanding and also to see if clarifications are needed.

## Self-Ranking Strategies

A good way to quickly check for understanding before or during a lesson is to use an easy ranking strategy. Students can show with their hands how competent they feel about the lesson topic. This technique requires a classroom climate where students feel comfortable demonstrating their level of understanding. For example, some students might have trouble admitting that they are confused about a concept that is presented. The teacher should discuss the importance of admitting misunderstandings and seeking help. It is also important for students to be respectful and realize that everyone has areas of strengths and weaknesses.

## Finger Rating 1–5

Have students hold up fingers to show their level of understanding.

5. Very clear—I can explain to someone else.
4. Clear—I understand.

3. Mostly clear—I understand almost all.
2. Not very clear—I don't understand.
1. Unclear—I don't understand at all.

*Thumbs Rating — Up/Middle/Down*

Thumbs up—I understand.
Thumbs sideways—I have some confusion.
Thumbs down—I do not understand.

*Error Analysis*

*Materials: Lesson content that contains some deliberate errors*

"What's wrong with this picture?" Remember hearing this phrase? It harks back to the classic mind puzzles where one tries to figure out the mistake or identify something missing in a picture. Error analysis requires close examination and the ability to know what is right in order to know why something is *not* right.

Clarifying understanding through error analysis is another one of those high-powered teaching tools. It's a perfect strategy for *during learning assessments*. When a teacher stops and shows two examples of a previously learned concept, where one is correct and one has an error, the wheels start turning in students' heads.

Say, for instance, a teacher just explained how to safely set up a science experiment. She might then show two examples of the equipment, one set up correctly and one incorrectly. The students then talk in pairs or small groups and determine which is the incorrect setup and explain why it is a problem.

*Truth or Lie Game*

*Materials: Index cards, pencils*

After a lesson chunk of information, stop and clarify understanding by briefly playing the Truth or Lie Game. Give each student an index card and have them space out the numbers 1–3 on the card. Ask the students to think of three statements about something they just learned in the lesson. What they want to do is create two statements that are true and one that is false (the lie). Be sure that they hide the lie randomly so that the false statement could be first, second, or third in the list.

Next, have students stand up and walk around with their cards. Use a whistle or special sound to indicate when they stop and find a partner. Students share cards with a partner and each person tries to find the lie. Randomly ask a few partners to tell the lie they found and how they could change the false item into a fact. Have students mingle a few times and find different partners to find the lies. Be sure to look for any incorrect assumptions and make clarifications.

## OOPS!

*Materials: A set of facts or pictures related to the current lesson topic that has some errors in them*

A great way to clarify misconceptions is to actually show misconceptions. All learners occasionally have those "oops" moments where they leave out a step in a math process or forget a syntax rule in writing. Students enjoy playing detective and determining what's wrong.

Create a set of slides with some specific examples of the lesson content where there are a few errors in the examples. Try to have a variety of errors that show a broad range of problems, with some easy to spot and others more subtle and tricky.

## Three Heads Together

*Materials: Key lesson vocabulary words/phrases written on a chart or board*

This activity takes just a few minutes and is a good way to break up a lesson. Have students work in groups of three and ask them to decide who is number one, two, and three. Create a numbered list of three review words from a recent lesson on the board. Each person in the group uses the word that corresponds to their number and tries to explain it to the other two. Students in the group help each other clarify the words if needed. Randomly check the groups for explanations of the words. Check for correct meanings and any misunderstandings.

## Stand Up Review

*Materials: None unless you want some sort of an audible signal such as a bell or whistle to indicate time to begin/share/stop*

Many times during a lesson, students just need a break and a chance to stand up and walk around for a few minutes. Quick breaks like these can serve a dual purpose: they can provide opportunities for movement and they can be a way to briefly review lesson content. For this strategy, stop the lesson at a crucial point to review concepts that have just been taught. Ask all the students to stand up, walk around, and mingle.

Give the students some time to mingle, then give a signal that it's time to find a partner. Have the pairs talk and share things that were clear about the lesson so far and one thing that might need clarification. Next, signal that it's time to stop. Randomly pick pairs to share what they talked about and encourage them to focus on anything that was confusing. A good idea is to have another student clarify the misconception. This creates valuable opportunities to review and clear up misunderstandings, especially if several students are confused.

## Choice Review

*Materials: Choice templates (See 4.5 mini choice menus on the book's companion website), writing tools*

Providing choice is a proven way to increase student participation and engagement. It is important to have opportunities for students to use their strengths/talents to show their understanding. During a lesson, stop and prompt students to summarize what they just learned by allowing them to select a response option such as writing, drawing, talking, or even singing or rapping (see sample choice menus on the book's companion website). These interludes can add some enjoyment to the learning process and also create a new memory pathway for students to retain the information.

The teacher can manage this activity by setting some ground rules, such as time to create the response (3–5 minutes), and establishing a process for sharing. Teachers might choose a few volunteers and/or randomly select student names (see name randomizer tools on the book's companion website) to share examples of lesson reviews.

## Quick Draw and Guess

*Materials: Paper or mini-white board and drawing tools, small slips of paper with two to three key words (different words for each partner in the pair)*

Many teachers and students will be familiar with the classic game of Pictionary in which a player must draw a visual representation of a given word, then players must try to guess the word. This formative assessment strategy works like Pictionary. The students will need to work in pairs. After a lesson, choose four to six key academic vocabulary terms from the lesson. Prepare slips of paper with about two different vocabulary terms for each of the two students in the pair. A good idea is to fold the slips of paper so that the words are hidden. The pair will also need paper and a drawing tool or a mini dry erase board and a marker.

The teacher gives a signal to start the review. Partner #1 chooses a word and creates a visual about the term. On the next signal, partner #1 shows the visual to partner #2 to try to guess the word. Give the students a few minutes to guess and then let them share the actual word and the meaning. To continue the activity, switch turns so that partner #2 creates the next visual with a different word.

Be sure to take time to summarize the word meanings and clarify any misunderstandings. As an extension of this activity, have students vote on visuals that best represent key academic vocabulary, then post them as mnemonic tools or references for the class.

*What Did Your Partner Say?*

*Materials: Slides or chart with open-ended review questions about the lesson content, academic conversation prompts (See 4.6 conversation prompts on the book's companion website.)*

This activity is a good way to get students to improve their listening skills. The review focuses on listening to a partner's explanation and asking questions. To make this activity as effective and powerful as possible, the teacher should model active listening before having students pair off.

In this review strategy, students work in pairs and take turns listening to one another, answering open-ended review questions that can be provided by the teacher. Partner #1 must listen to partner #2 answer questions. If needed, partner #2 can ask questions for confirmation or clarification (see the academic conversation prompts). Then, partner #1 uses his or her own words to retell what they heard from partner #2. Emphasize that students should avoid repeating exactly what their partners said.

Make sure that students understand that you will be randomly calling on them to tell what they heard. These random checks help add accountability. Asking students to tell what they *heard*, not what they said, can strengthen and increase both active listening and oral summarizing skills.

## After Learning

In the hustle and bustle of teaching, it is easy for teachers to lose track of time, look at the clock, and realize that the lesson must end quickly. When this occurs, a teacher might be inclined to remind students about homework or something due the next day. But such hastiness can cause a teacher to leave out a critical component of learning. It is imperative to bring together the ideas of the day's learning by clarifying and summarizing what was just learned.

To accomplish this, simply go back to the lesson's objective or learning target and ask the students to explain key learning goals. Another idea is to have each student complete a *ticket-out-the-door* that requires students to respond to a review question. The following items offer ideas for innovative strategies that can add variety to this critical learning phase of lesson appraisal.

## After-Learning Strategies

*Easiest/Hardest or Clearest/Cloudiest*

*Materials: Slips of paper and writing tools (See 4.7 clear or cloudy [two on a page] handout on the book's companion website.)*

When students are summarizing a lesson, it is important to gather information about what they understood and what remains confusing. One way to gather this information is by asking students to explain what elements of the lesson were easiest or clearest to them and then which things were the most difficult or cloudy for them. There are several ways to address the findings.

One way is to collect student responses, quickly tally the results, and share with students at the beginning of the next lesson. Another technique is to have students jot down what was easiest/hardest and take time to share and discuss their responses as a class at the end of the lesson. Regardless of the approach, emphasize the importance of student feedback and remind students that the teacher's goal is to ensure that key lesson concepts are clear. Additionally, the teacher should remediate learning for students who are struggling.

*Give Me Five*

*Materials: Paper and writing tool to trace hand*

To add variety to the summarizing process, try this *Give Me Five* activity. Amazingly, students of all ages seem to like this strategy. Have the students place one hand flat on a piece of paper and trace the shape of their hand. Next, prompt each student to think of five key things that they remember about the lesson and write one thing on each finger. Examples include a vocabulary word, a concept, or a visual.

Randomly choose some students to share what they wrote as a lesson review. Another idea is to have the students recall the main idea of the lesson and write that on the palm of the hand. Distribute the Give Me Five summaries at the beginning of the next lesson and use them as a quick review of previous learning.

*What's the Takeaway?*

*Materials: Paper and writing tools*

Another quick way for students to summarize a lesson is to have them identify the key concepts, or the big *takeaways*. Start by having each student jot down one key concept that they learned in the lesson. Encourage students to describe new information they learned or describe a new understanding of an already familiar concept. Next have students share their takeaways in pairs or small groups. Then, as a whole group, share the takeaways, record student feedback, and clarify any fallacies in understanding. A good technique is to refer back to this class review the following day to refresh their memories of the previous learning.

*Doors to Your Mind*

*Materials: Paper and writing tools, preferably a pencil for lighter marks (See 4.8 doors to your mind handout on the book's companion website.)*

This activity is a way for students to generate review questions about lesson content. Students will be creating a three-flap foldable, where each flap represents a door. The student directions that can be used with the handout or modeled from the graphic are shown in figure 4.6.

## Student Directions for Doors to Your Mind Summarizing Activity

1. Think about what you learned today.
2. Fold a piece of paper in half the long way. Next make two cuts so that you have three flaps. Each of the three flaps should open and close. Each flap represents one door.
3. Think of challenging questions related to today's lesson. Write a different lesson review question on the front of each of the three flaps or doors.
4. Next, write the answer to the question behind the flap or door (write lightly or use a pencil).
5. After you have three questions and three answers, work with a partner.
6. Take turns. Let your partner choose a door. Ask the question. See if your partner's answer matches the answer behind the door.
7. Clarify the reasoning for your answers.

This is an activity that can be duplicated with several different pairs of students since they may have different review questions.

## Anytime Learning

Most instructional strategies, like the ones included previously in this chapter, can be adapted for use during various stages of learning. However, there are some instructional approaches that are more adaptable. The following strategies can easily be adjusted to check for background knowledge, a mid-lesson checkpoint, or a final lesson summarizer.

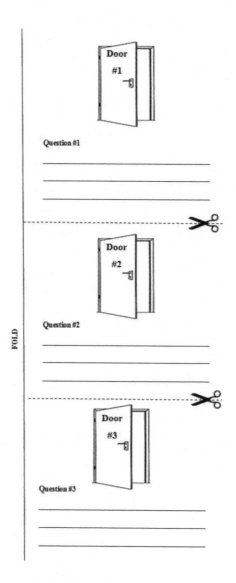

**Figure 4.6.   Doors to your mind review.**

## Anytime-Learning Strategies

*Pair, Compare, and Share*

*Materials: Paper, pencils, and large recording board*

This interactive strategy provides an opportunity for students to move around, interact with peers, and share information at any stage of the learning process. This activity is adapted from Spencer Kagan's (1994) structure, "Give One, Get One," as part of his cooperative learning strategies. To begin, give each student one piece of blank paper. Model how to fold the paper into squares, such as six or nine squares (see figure 4.7).

Next, explain that the object of the activity is to write a different word or phrase about the topic in each box on the paper. First, present the topic to the students. For example, when doing a lesson review, the teacher might say, "Choose one box on your paper and write down an important word or phrase that you learned in the lesson."

Next, model how the students will *Pair, Compare, and Share* their papers. Have two students demonstrate how they would pair and compare each other's papers. If they have different ideas, they can share by writing the idea they got in a new box on their paper. They would then pair with another person and follow the same procedure of comparing and sharing. The goal is to fill each box on the paper with a different word/phrase.

After modeling the process, have all the students stand up and walk around and begin collecting words to fill up their papers. When they are done, have them sit in small groups. Select a volunteer who is also a fast writer to come to the front. Go around to each group and have students give one word from their paper while the fast writer records the word on the board.

Keep going around to all the groups, trying to choose different people. Students cannot repeat a word that has already been written on the board.

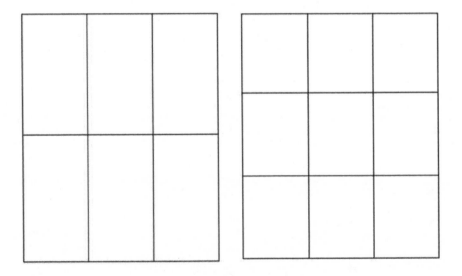

**Figure 4.7.    2-by-3 and 3-by-3 grids for Pair, Compare, and Share.**

Finally, look over the words and see what kinds of themes are represented. Is there anything on the list that might represent a misconception? If so, support the students in making clarifications.

## *"No Voices" Brainstorming*

*Materials: Large pieces of paper like butcher-block paper, writing tools such as markers and pens, and content questions to place in the center of the papers.*

Sometimes it's a good idea to add a novel twist to an instructional strategy. For this task, students walk around and draw or write responses to questions without talking. To prepare for the activity, have three to five broad open-ended questions written or attached to the center of the large paper. Use questions that will elicit prior knowledge or provide a review about a topic. For example, before a class study of the novel *The Giver* ask the students broad questions such as:

1. When is it better to be part of a group than it is to be alone?
2. What are examples of the past repeating itself?
3. Should you ever experience cold or hunger? Why?

Explain the directions for the activity. Students will divide into three groups and walk around to each paper, read the question, and look at the responses from others in the group. Students can add a reply (pro, con, or clarification) to another student's response. Rotate the groups so that each group has about three to five minutes for each question. Lastly, bring the sheets to the front of the room and share some themes that came out of the responses.

## *Show What You Know*

*Materials: Any writing tool and paper/wipe-off board/plastic sheet cover*

Teachers can get total class participation and check for understanding by using a variety of *Show Me* techniques. In this strategy, the teacher can ask any type of question. Students then write their answers on paper or wipe-off boards and hold them up for the teacher to see.

Teachers can also give each student letters such as *A, B, C,* or *D,* then show a multiple-choice question with four possible choices such as *A, B, C,* or *D.* A good strategy is for students to keep the letters face down on their desk. Students should hold up cards indicating the letter (*A, B, C,* or *D*) that they think is the right answer. Discuss and clarify the correct answer. This strategy also works with True/False questions where students show a *T* or *F*.

**Tip:** Have students use two hands to show their answer. One hand holds the answer card and the other covers the answer. Then when the teacher gives the signal, students uncover the answer. This keeps students from looking around at other answers instead of making their own decision about the correct answer.

Another idea is the use of small wipe-off (or dry erase) boards. When students show their board in response to a teacher question during a lesson, the teacher knows right away who understands and who still needs help. A teacher can instantly change the direction of a lesson or re-teach based on this feedback.

**Tip:** A cheaper variation of the wipe-off board is using a blank piece of paper inside a clear plastic sheet protector.

Here are some suggestions for *Show Me* strategies:

- Multiple choice questions
- True/false questions
- Draw/visualize a response
- Show mathematical work
- Partner share—two students and one board—one works and one checks, then switch

*Face-Off Game*

*Materials: Any writing tool and paper/wipe-off board/plastic sheet cover and task cards with content questions*

Divide the class into small groups of four or five students. Give each member a wipe-off board and group task cards. Have each group determine a group leader and a group summary recorder. Give each group leader a set of task cards that are placed face down in the center of the group. The group recorder will need one piece of paper to record summaries. Every student is given a wipe-off board and dry erase marker.

The group leader begins by showing the first task card, after which the students write their response on their board. When they are finished, they put their boards face down until everyone is finished. Then the group leader says "Face-Off" and everyone in the group shows their responses and compares answers. The group decides on a summary for the first task and the group recorder writes it down. The process continues until all the task cards have been completed.

*Mini-Writes*

*Materials: Paper and writing tools (See 4.9 mini-write rubric [two on a page] on the book's companion website.)*

Short writing tasks, or *Mini-Writes*, can be used to informally assess student thinking, develop writing fluency, and build the habit of reflection. In this strategy, the teacher asks students to respond in 2–10 minutes to an open-ended question or prompt posed by the teacher before, during, or after a lesson or reading assignment.

Here are some ways the strategy might be used:

- Activating prior knowledge by preparing students for reading, writing, or discussing
- Encouraging students to make personal connections
- Promoting reflection about key concepts from the lesson content
- Summarizing the main points from the teacher's direct instruction
- Stimulating critical thinking by analyzing or evaluating concepts
- Organizing key details from a larger concept

Select a topic that is related to the lesson and define the purpose for the Mini-Write, such as finding out what students already know, reviewing what was just heard, or summarizing main ideas using key academic vocabulary. Stress that in a Mini-Write, students will respond to a question or prompt related to the lesson by writing down whatever comes to mind without organizing it too much or worrying about spelling and/or grammar. The teacher should also share the qualities of an effective Mini-Write, which include focusing on the content topic, using content vocabulary, and actively writing. If using a self-assessment rubric, the teacher should share the rubric with the students ahead of time.

When first using this instructive assessment technique, teachers will find it helpful to provide students with criteria that describe the elements within an effective quick reflective writing piece. The rubric in table 4.1 is an example of a helpful tool for student self-assessment or peer-assessment of Mini-Writes. One additional strategy that can be used with the rubric is using a highlighting marker to validate ratings. For example, the student can highlight the academic vocabulary and the content details used in the Mini-Write, which would confirm the rubric rating.

## Electronic Tools for Instructive Assessment

*Note: These tools are hyperlinked on the book's companion website.*

Most of the examples thus far have been strategies for students to write/converse/collaborate about their understandings of lesson content. However, there are many more up-to-date and useful electronic tools that can quickly collect and even tabulate student understandings. A few of the most popular ones are listed. All of these are tools that the authors have used or have seen classroom teachers use successfully.

One challenge with these amazing online tools is that students will need electronic devices with web access. Some schools have sets of tablets or laptops that students can use, or some teachers ask students to "Bring Your

**Table 4.1.   Rubric for Self and/or Peer Assessment of a Mini-Write**

|  | Exceptional | Adequate | Developing | Needs Work |
|---|---|---|---|---|
| Vocabulary | I used three or more key vocabulary words in my explanation. | I used two key vocabulary words in my explanation. | I used one key vocabulary word in my explanation. | I did not use any new vocabulary words. |
| Content Details | I gave several specific content details that brought the topic to life. | I gave some specific content details. | I gave only a few details. | I did not give much detail at all. |
| Focus | I was very engaged in the writing process. I was actively working the entire time. | I was engaged in the writing process. I was actively working most of the time. | I was somewhat engaged in the writing process. I was working some of the time. | I had a lot of difficulty being engaged in the writing process. I had a hard time with this task. |

Own Device" (BYOD). Another solution for classes in which students do not have access to electronic devices is to use Plickers (see description below).

*Answer Garden: https://answergarden.ch/*

Answer Garden is a quick one-question response tool. It has a very minimalist format so that teachers can use it to establish the knowledge level of their class on a certain topic. Students can submit answers using any type of device. The responses show up on the teacher's screen in the form of a word cloud. Responses that are submitted by more than one person are shown in larger font. It is free and easy to use. It would also be helpful for self-evaluation with questions like "Which part of the lesson was most challenging for you?"

*Padlet: https://padlet.com/ (formerly known as Wallwisher)*

This online tool allows teachers to create an interactive bulletin board or wall. Students can respond to a question or topic by posting a message that looks like a sticky note. The wall can be printed out for the teacher to see the extent of class knowledge on a topic. Students can add images, videos, and documents to their post, using any device.

The basic version is free but there are premier versions that require a subscription. Beyond formative assessment, students can also add information they have learned about content. For example, one class studying deserts found information about various deserts and created an electronic bulletin board. See this example: https://padlet.com/kferrell/deserts

*Socrative: http://www.socrative.com/*

This app is a great way to gain insight into student learning with easy-to-create quizzes, polls, and tickets-out-the-door. This tool provides an alternative to the more expensive electronic clickers and is easy to set up and use. There is a free basic version or a pro version available for a minimal fee. In addition, the Socrative website has a blog with ideas for using the tool and a section where teachers share quizzes they have made.

*Plickers: https://plickers.com/ (students hold up cards rather than use a device)*

Plickers is a free online tool that lets teachers collect real-time formative assessment data without the need for student devices. The way it works is that each student is given a card with a unique visual code. The code has four sides, each lettered *A*, *B*, *C*, and *D*. Teachers use an app on their cellphones to slowly scan student cards around the room. The app recognizes the cards, then records the name and response of each student. The cards are free to print out from the Plickers website or commercial Plickers cards can be purchased from Amazon.

## Additional Resources (Check out the book's companion website for recent updates.)

There are several great websites that have compiled the best electronic formative assessment tools:

1. Growing the List: 50 Digital Education Tools and Apps for Formative Assessment. https://www.nwea.org/blog/2015/growing-list-50-digital-education-tools-apps-formative-assessment-success/
2. Five Fantastic, Fast, Formative Assessment Tools. https://www.edutopia.org/blog/5-fast-formative-assessment-tools-vicki-davis
3. Thirteen Tools Teachers Would Love for Formative Assessment. http://edtechreview.in/trends-insights/insights/1766-tools-teachers-would-love-for-formative-assessments
4. Take Three! 55 Digital Tools and Apps for Formative Assessment Success. https://www.nwea.org/blog/2016/take-three-55-digital-tools-and-apps-for-formative-assessment-success/

## POST-READING QUESTIONS

The following questions were listed at the beginning of this chapter for readers to contemplate prior to reading this chapter. The same questions are listed a second time, followed by commentary from the authors' perspective.

- What comes to your mind when you hear the term *instructive assessment*?
- How would you describe the benefits of formative assessments to students . . . to teachers?
- How would formative assessments vary based on the stage of learning?
- Should formative assessments be graded?
- How are you increasing your use of formative assessment techniques?

## POST-READING QUESTIONS

**What comes to mind when you hear the term *instructive assessment*?** Hopefully, by now, the *instructive* part of assessment is clear. The term *instructive assessment* is used synonymously with the phrase *formative assessment*. The reason that we chose to use *instructive* instead of *formative* was to emphasize the power of formative assessment to *instruct* the student and the teacher about the efficacy of the teaching and learning that happens on a daily basis. Well-designed instructive assessments result in more reflective and refined teaching, provide more specific feedback to students, and impact learners to become more self-aware of their own strengths and areas for growth.

**Describe the benefits of formative assessments to students . . . to teachers?** The benefits of formative assessment have been proven both anecdotally and empirically. According to Chappuis and Chappuis (2007), some of the distinct benefits of formative assessment include:

- The timeliness of results enables teachers to adjust instruction quickly, while learning is in progress.
- The students who are assessed are the ones who benefit from the adjustments.
- The students can use the results to adjust and improve their own learning (p. 18).

In very simple terms, instructive assessments, unlike summative assessments, allow students and teachers to form more detailed understandings of student abilities, which can inform remediation, re-teaching, and instructional techniques.

**How would formative assessments vary based on the stage of learning?** In this chapter, a strong case was made for teachers to have a variety of formative assessment strategies that can be applied in all types of instructional settings. When students are in the initial stages of learning a new skill, formative techniques need to be more frequent and more specifically aligned to the learning targets. As the skill is expanded and students become more proficient, then the formative assessments can become more self-evaluative and reflective in nature.

**Should formative assessments be graded?** The consensus of most educational experts is that is it detrimental to assign a grade to a formative assessment. During the initial stages of learning, the student is still in the practice mode. We wouldn't want a score to count in a sports practice session. Likewise, when a grade is assigned to a task that students are just beginning to grasp, it dishonors the learning process. The grade puts a final stamp on the assignment and can actually shut down the willingness of the student to use feedback and self-reflect.

Savvy teachers are finding ways to get around the grading of formative assessments. They may give a grade as a temporary marker that gets changed after the summative assessment is given. Other teachers may just give a check for completing the task, or they may weigh the formative assessment much lower when determining a student's final average.

Whatever the case, students need to feel comfortable in taking risks and making mistakes. Some of the best learning happens when students struggle first with misunderstandings but eventually reach clarity.

**How are you increasing your use of formative assessment techniques?** The goal of this chapter was to expand teachers' thinking and usage of instructive assessment. Like the saying "variety is the spice of life," strategic use of a variety of formative assessments creates spicy learning for students.

## REFERENCES

Black, P., & Wiliam, D. (1998). Inside the black box: Raising standards through classroom assessment. *Phi Delta Kappan, 80*(2), 139–148.

Brookhart, S. (2008). *How to give effective feedback to your students.* Alexandria, VA: ASCD.

Chappuis, S., & Chappuis, J. (2007). The best value in formative assessment. *Educational Leadership, 65*(4), 14–18.

Jensen, E. (1998). *Teaching with the brain in mind.* Alexandria, VA: ASCD.

Kagan, S., & Kagan, M. (1994). *Kagan cooperative learning.* San Clemente, CA: Kagan Publishing.

Marzano, R. J., & Brown, J. L. (2009). *A handbook for the art and science of teaching.* Alexandria, VA: ASCD.

Rowe, M. B. (1986). Wait time: Slowing down may be a way of speeding up! *Journal of Teacher Education, 23,* 43–49.

Stiggins, R. J., Arter, J., Chappuis, J., & Chappuis, S. (2006). *Classroom assessment for student learning: Doing it right—using it well.* Portland, OR: Assessment Training Institute.

Wiliam, D. (2011). What is assessment for learning? *Studies in Educational Evaluation, 37*(1), 3–14.

*Chapter Five*

# Solution Three

*Provide Active Student Ownership of Assessment*

"It's a paradox. When teachers hand over to students the power to shape their own learning, the learning that occurs is often more powerful than what would have transpired if the teacher had directed learning activities. Even the most effective teacher can't do students' learning for them."—Susan Brookhart, Connie Moss, and Beverly Long

## PRE-READING QUESTIONS

Before reading this chapter, it may be helpful to consider your prior knowledge and/or opinions regarding the following questions:

1. What is the value in having students self-assess their own learning?
2. What student dispositions are helpful for effective self-assessment?
3. How can you create learning environments conducive to student ownership of assessment?
4. What are some of the challenges and benefits of peer assessment?
5. How can you add depth and variety to self or peer assessments?

After completing chapter 5, you can revisit these questions and review some final commentary from the authors. See the section Post-Reading Questions near the end of the chapter.

# INTRODUCTION

Imagine the following scenarios: A student just finished a two-week research project and turns in the assignment to be graded. A few days later, she receives a grade of 77 and letter grade of C. Not surprisingly she wonders, "Why the grade of C?" or "What could be done to improve?" Alternatively, another student completes a choice assignment in which he selects the type of materials and strategies to create his own invention. He looks at the rubric prior to the task and knows exactly what the expectations will be.

Before turning in his work, he looks over the rubric and grades himself. He feels confident that he will earn a high B. After some self-reflection, this student accepts the fact that there might have even been the possibility to earn an A if his work had been planned ahead and not so rushed at the end.

In the first scenario, the teacher owned the assessment; in the second, the student *and* the teacher shared ownership.

This chapter focuses on student ownership of assessment. Recall that chapter 2 introduced student ownership of the assessment process and emphasized the importance of providing clear instructional goals, which empower students to self-assess capabilities in achieving those aims. Additionally, data dialogue was presented as an instructional strategy that promotes student understanding of content area expectations, individual strengths, and individual needs for mastering learning targets.

What was not covered in chapter 2 was the nuts and bolts of the background reasoning for self or peer assessment and specific strategies that teachers can employ to promote more active, relevant, and purposeful student evaluation of learning.

## IMPORTANCE OF ACTIVE STUDENT PARTICIPATION IN THE EVALUATION PROCESS

There is an old saying from past agrarian times—you can lead a horse to water, but you can't make him drink. The message for education in this saying is that one can encourage, prod, pressure, and even plead with a student to study and learn, but it is eventually the student who makes the internal motivating decision to actually want to learn.

Teachers can even use external rewards to promote student interest in learning, but ultimately the learner is the one who must take ownership of the learning process. In addition, active self-evaluation nurtures student dispositions to face the challenges of college and/or career and future problems life might throw at them.

# FOUR STUDENT CHARACTERISTICS NURTURED THROUGH SELF-ASSESSMENT

## 1. Intrinsic Motivation: Students Having a Desire to Improve Their Learning

A quote attributed to Aristotle goes like this: "Each human being is bred with a unique set of potentials that yearn to be fulfilled as surely as the acorn yearns to become the oak within it." Most people inherently yearn to be competent. A person doesn't typically get up in the morning and say, "I think I will be incompetent today." However, the forces of daily living, along with challenges and frustrations, can get in the way, and personal motivation might fall to the wayside.

For the past 30 years or more, cognitive psychologists have explored and researched the complex phenomenon of internal motivation. What is it that drives a person to want to tackle a task or learn a new skill? Some of the interesting research on motivation, especially in terms of education, focuses on the difference between intrinsic and extrinsic motivation.

So, for example, with extrinsic motivation, students tend to do tasks mainly because doing so will produce some kind of reward or outside advantage upon completion. In contrast, with intrinsic motivation, students are doing the tasks because they have the personal desire or they view the tasks as enjoyable, applicable, or challenging to them.

Over the years, numerous authors and researchers have examined this issue of internal versus external motivation. In 2014, a group of researchers led by Genevieve Taylor conducted an extensive meta-analysis and determined that intrinsic motivation was consistently positively associated with academic achievement (Taylor et al., 2014). It appears that long-lasting learning that transfers to advancement in life skills happens to a greater extent via intrinsic motivation.

In a school culture that focuses on students getting external rewards for doing tasks (e.g., stickers, certificates, grades), it is not surprising that it is a challenge for students and teachers to see the benefits of self-assessment. Alfie Kohn's book, *Punished by Rewards*, makes a strong case for dropping the old technique of the persistent dangling carrot. He advocates alternatively that teachers support students in developing internal motivation by designing and implementing meaningful tasks and choice assignments.

Here's where teachers will need to do self-reflecting as well. They will need to consider how intrinsic motivation ultimately empowers the student.

## 2. Autonomy: Students Taking Ownership of Their Learning

Teachers can employ certain techniques that promote self-motivating behaviors in students so that they can take ownership of their learning. Many times, these strategies relate to encouraging a sense of autonomy and personal responsibility. Researcher and theorist Johnmarshall Reeve calls this type of pedagogy *autonomy-supportive teaching.*

Reeve's work is an off-shoot of the extensive literature and research on self-determination theory (SDT) by Ryan and Deci (2000). SDT purports that for personal well-being, people need to experience a sense of these three elements: autonomy, competence, and relatedness. (See more on SDT in the chapter notes.)

Autonomy supportive teachers tend to be more student focused and serve as facilitators in the learning process. They take into consideration factors such as student preferences and avoid the overuse of external techniques to control students with rewards or compliance demands. These teachers avoid controlling language that might coerce a student into submission. They also provide rationales to their students so that students know why particular expectations are being required. In short, teachers who support students in these ways are promoting the development of learners who will more aptly take ownership of their learning.

## 3. Metacognitive Thinking: Students Reflecting on Their Learning

Metacognition is a factor that can contribute to a student's ability to self-assess. Students must be able to think about their own thinking. They need the mental ability to reflectively know what they know and don't know and to be conscious of their own thought processes especially in problem-solving scenarios.

Young people need to hear adults talk about how they have reflected on their own thinking and weighed issues back and forth in their minds. When a student has a concern, a helpful response from a teacher would be to ask the student, "What have you already been thinking about this problem?" or "What are your thoughts about how the problem might be tackled?" The teacher needs to let students begin their own brainstorming, so they realize that, yes, they do have the capacity to solve their own problems.

Of course, metacognitive thinking skills may not come naturally for all students, especially young learners. On one hand, young children often have some of their own reflective thoughts and even outwardly speak their inner language, especially during imaginative play. However, deeper metacognitive thinking is thought to appear in the early stages of more formal thought at around age ten or eleven.

In any event, the process of self-assessing takes some level of personal self-reflection and metacognitive awareness. The more comfortable students become with self-assessment, the more they begin to honestly question themselves and openly look at their own abilities and capacities for learning, relearning, and sometimes even unlearning.

## 4. Resilience: Students Having the Persistence to Improve Their Learning

Extensive educational research on the habits of successful learners has focused on the personality trait of resilience (Condly, 2006). Resilience is thought to be the capacity to persist—to stick with a task and move forward despite numerous obstacles obstructing the path.

During self-assessment, students may become aware that they are not meeting their grade-level learning objectives and need to seek help. Students who lack resilience might give up. Other students might rate themselves higher or lower than their actual ability. Part of students' resilience is the capacity to face adversity head-on, as well as having the humility to admit that they have areas of needed growth. This can be an incredible challenge for students who have not received positive feedback about their natural abilities in the past or who exhibit a sense of learned helplessness.

Teachers can support the development of resilience by talking about this quality and giving personal examples of the value of struggle and persistence. The authors observed a language arts, middle-grade teacher who used stories of famous young athletes, actors, musicians, and inventors who had overcome immense personal adversity to thrive and succeed. The teacher used these examples to showcase how resilient behaviors could build character and advance the will to overcome academic challenge. As an additional tool, students were given problem-solving strategies for various writing challenges.

As part of the teacher's writing self-assessment criteria, reflective questions were built in that asked students questions such as "What type of struggle did you experience in this task?" and "What is a strategy you can use to overcome the struggle?" or "How can you move forward to tackle the challenge?" Questions like these point to the elements of resilience needed for open and honest self-assessment that can develop from valuing the struggle.

SETTING THE STAGE FOR SELF-ASSESSMENT

## A Classroom Climate That Supports Self-Assessment

In chapter 2, the issue of classroom climate was discussed, as well as the importance of establishing and nurturing a classroom environment that is accepting and inviting for all students. This positive climate is even more critical when it comes to the prospect of learner-owned assessment. Learners need to feel a sense of trust so that they can reveal their learning strengths and needs and have these revelations be accepted and honored by the class community.

Students need to know that like anything in life, every person has some areas where they will shine and some areas where they will fall behind and need additional support or encouragement. Being open and honest is the best policy for establishing the framework and relationships needed for self-assessments.

Before beginning any self-assessment or peer-assessment techniques, it is critical to have discussions with the group about the value of these types of assessment. How do they benefit learning? What do they look like? Are they graded? There are, no doubt, many more burning questions that students will offer.

## Issues of Power

In designing and implementing effective self-assessment techniques, the teacher should be aware of power differentials. Who ultimately has the power over student learning and achievement outcomes? In environments where teachers and students are made to feel that assessment is primarily a heavy-handed element of authority that is constantly looking down on them with a microscope and demanding results, self-assessment might seem unimportant or even unthinkable.

When the power of assessment is given to the student, there can be a sense of freedom and empowerment in this new sense of ownership. Students may ponder, "So I am the one who owns my work?" If this type of ownership has not been experienced before, get ready for some uncomfortable feelings and perhaps even pushback about self-evaluation.

CHALLENGES/CAUTIONS

## The Timing of Self-Assessment

Here are some words of caution about how self-assessment complements various stages of learning. First, to be able to self-assess, students need some sense of what "good" looks like. For example, if you ask students to self-assess a piece of narrative writing and the students haven't consistently heard, seen, or read good models of effective narratives, then how can they know the criteria on which to base their own self-assessment?

Usually self-assessment fits in best after students have had some exposure to the elements of a concept, so they know the basic key components and have been given some examples of tasks related to the concepts. Remember, students need enough knowledge of a topic to be able to effectively self-assess.

## Modeling the Process of Self-Assessment

One piece of learning that teachers can easily forget is the powerful element of modeling a process. Teachers become so familiar with, and expert in, content knowledge that they can forget what the learning process for a concept looks like to novice learners. Just as an expert sculptor apprentices a beginning sculptor by modeling and scaffolding the crafting of a sculpture, so, too, can teachers support their apprentices by showing the steps that an expert takes in the process of self-assessment.

Recently, in an observation in a third-grade classroom, a teacher expertly modeled the process of self-assessment in a learning segment on creating and analyzing data the students had collected. The teacher used as a model a sample product from a previous student and self-assessed the work as if it were her own. A *think-aloud* strategy was used to explain how to self-assess the various components and criteria of the graphing task. The teacher said, for example, "I see that I did a very good job labeling the axis on the bar graph, but the grid lines I created are not equal and it makes my results look wrong."

Another helpful modeling strategy for self-assessing is providing a real-life demonstration of self-assessment. After the teacher observes the students self-assess or peer-assess in an effective manner, she could have them create a short skit to act out the process for the rest of the class. Alternatively, the teacher could create a script of an effective self- or peer-assessment scenario. There are always some budding actors in a group who are more than willing to perform.

When students see what good self-assessing looks and sounds like, they can begin to emulate this process. Notice in the third-grade example, the teacher modeled how self-assessment has both "glows and grows" for the learner. Remember this key point: Self-assessment is the self-analysis of a task, noting what was done well and what needs improvement.

## Differentiating Self-Assessment

Educators realize that there rarely is a one-size-fits-all solution to any instructional strategy. Therefore, self-assessment, like any other learning technique, needs some level of differentiation. Struggling learners, especially older ones who may have experienced a cycle of persistent underachievement, may need help knowing how to realistically, accurately, and caringly assess their own strengths and areas for improvement. Likewise, overachieving students may either be too hard on themselves or be overconfident about their own capabilities.

It is crucial for teachers to know the varied levels of knowledge, metacognition, confidence, and resilience that students bring to the self-assessment process. That's why teachers need to frame self-assessment with discussions about the "why" of the process. Students should clearly know what's in it for them to self-assess their own work. In the student assessment strategies that follow, some suggestions are included for ways to modify the strategies for various abilities and personalities.

## Peer Assessment Cautions

Over the years both authors have practiced a variety of techniques in using peer assessment. Some of these experiences have been positive and effective and others have proven calamitous. It seems that effective peer assessment requires several elements: a clarified purpose, clear guidelines, modeling, and some agreed-upon criteria for the assessment. The teacher should also consider the way in which peers will be selected to evaluate each other.

It's obvious that some student pairing just does not work out. There could be a variety of reasons, including personality clashes, broad or narrow ability spans, language barriers, or the fact that some students just feel uncomfortable assessing others. In addition, age is another factor. Young children at the early elementary level may not be developmentally ready for peer-assessment scenarios.

On the positive side, peer assessment can be a powerful tool. Sometimes a peer can give more effective feedback to others within their own age-level dialect. Almost all educators have experienced situations in which a student struggles with the teacher's explanation of a concept. Then, the teacher asks another student to explain it, and suddenly the struggling student exclaims, "Okay, now I get it!"

Just like self-assessment, peer assessment needs structure, a model, and a set of criteria. Throughout the next section of this chapter as self-assessment strategies are explored, there will be examples of ways to apply techniques for both self and peer assessment.

## Strategies for Self-Assessment

In a meta-analysis of the efficacy of self and peer assessments conducted by Sebba, Crick, Yu, Lawson, Harlen, and Durant (2008), researchers found that self-assessments showed a significant effect on learning outcomes in addition to positive impacts on student engagement and independence. Experienced teachers have come to realize that students who take ownership of their learning typically ask more questions and are more likely to be aware of their own strengths and shortcomings.

However, knowing that self-assessment has been shown to be efficacious is one thing, but having a variety of strategies and instructional options for implementing the process is another. Therefore, what follows is a plethora of techniques for teachers who may either be beginning to infuse self- or peer assessment into their instruction or for educators hoping to enhance their student self-assessment methods.

### Quick Self-Assessments

During instruction, teachers often need quick and easy ways to determine if students comprehend the lesson content or need clarification or additional support. By asking students to self-assess their level of understanding, teachers can quickly modify instruction and students can get the help they need. This happens in a classroom setting where the teacher has created a climate conducive to open, honest, and nonjudgmental interactions.

Refer to the quick self-ranking strategies in chapter 4 where students can use a *thumbs-up, thumbs-sideways, or thumbs-down* or a one to five finger rating to visually show the teacher how confident they feel about a skill that was demonstrated.

### Windshield Checks

*Materials: Writing tools, paper, or accompanying handout (See 5.1 windshield check handout on the book's companion website.)*
This is a strategy that has appeared in numerous instructional books and websites. The self-assessment strategy is shared here with some slight modifications. The strategy can be used as a mid-lesson checkpoint or as a *ticket-out-the-door*. The basic premise of this activity is for students to self-assess their level of clarity in understanding the lesson content so that the teacher knows how many students are ready to move forward or how many need more support. Students rate their level of clarity using the metaphor of a car windshield.

Example (see figure 5.1):

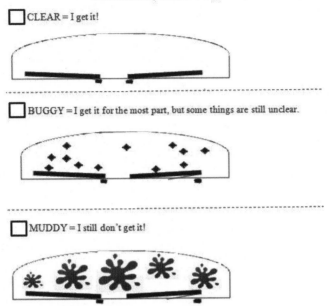

**Figure 5.1. Windshield check.**

- CLEAR = I get it!
- BUGGY = I get it for the most part, but some things are still unclear.
- MUDDY = I still don't get it!

This visual image of clear, buggy, or muddy understanding can be a lighthearted way to think about levels of understanding. Students can also write or discuss a justification for their rating. Of course, teachers should probe deeper to specifically determine those unclear concepts and work on clarification.

*Four Corners Check: Do You Get It?*

*Materials: Optional corner signs (See 5.2 four corners signs on the book's companion website.)*

This strategy is a good technique to use when teaching a new skill or concept. Teachers can pause after a beginning explanation of the topic and do a quick check to see if students are "getting it." Explain the four levels of understanding listed below:

Corner One: I don't get it at all.
Corner Two: I get some of it, but I still need help.
Corner Three: I get most of it, and I'm ready to move on.

Corner Four: I really get it and could teach others.

Ask students to go to a corner of the room that best represents how they are self-assessing their level of understanding. An important piece is for the teacher to first meet with groups one and four to clarify if they are in the right place. Students in each corner can begin to discuss components of the lesson and see which parts are clear and/or confusing to them. The teacher may want to match up some struggling students with those who can help explain the material. Depending on the level of understanding, the need for re-teaching can be determined.

## Highlighting / circling / color coding

*Materials: Lesson content materials that can be marked up either with highlighter pens or electronic highlighting tools; alternatively, teacher- or student-generated work can be placed inside a clear plastic protector sheet, and students can mark on top of the sheet as if it were a wipe-off board*

During a lesson, depending on the topic, students can circle or highlight areas of the content that they understand best and identify content that is most confusing. So, for example, a teacher might have a worksheet or student work sample on composing a short opinion piece in writing. The teacher might give students a list of key elements of opinion writing they have been studying such as using a strong argument or supplying specific supporting reasons. Students might highlight in yellow those elements that they were able to effectively demonstrate in their writing and then highlight in blue the areas of struggle.

This same technique could be used with peer review, where students are given specific criteria and then highlight examples of the criteria being effectively demonstrated and/or needing more work. This is a particularly helpful strategy since peers can highlight the evidence to clarify how they evaluated their peers' work.

## Where Am I on the Continuum? or "Take a Stand"

*Materials: A giant number line with numbers 1–10 on a strip of paper or tape attached to the center of the classroom floor, or placed in a hallway or outside, and a set of open-ended questions or statements that relate to class content; questions should either ask how well students understand something or how much they agree with a statement (See 5.3 labels for number line continuum or opinion on the book's companion website.)*

This activity is highly interactive since students all stand up and move to a self-selected position on a giant floor number line. For this activity to be successful, it is important for the teacher to set some ground rules. Explain that the line is going to be used for self-evaluation or self-reflecting. Below are examples:

Self-evaluating number line continuum:

1 = I do not understand at all.
5= I understand some.
10 = I understand completely.

Self-reflecting or opinion number line continuum:

1 = I don't agree at all.
5= I agree somewhat.
10 = I totally agree.

Students must listen carefully to the question or statement. Next, they move to the numbers on the number line that best represent their beliefs or opinions. It is helpful if the teacher has the questions/statements typed up ahead of time and projects them on a screen or whiteboard for the students to see. Teachers can even take a picture of student responses or have a student record the outcome of the surveys for each question.

The authors recently observed a ninth-grade social studies teacher use this continuum line with an activity on controversial governmental policies they had been studying. The students all started out standing near the middle of the line, and then the teacher projected a question on a slide for the students to see. After the students moved to their opinion position, the teacher selected a few students on opposing ends of the spectrum to justify their position. This activity was not only highly engaging but also allowed for some much-needed physical movement.

*Self-Reflection Guides*

*Materials: Paper and writing tools, optional sample self-reflection prompts for students (See 5.4 prompts for student self-reflection on the book's companion website.)*

Sometimes a good place to start with self-assessment is with the simple task of reflecting. Even young children can begin to understand the concept of evaluating their own opinion about a topic. "Did I like it? If so, why?" "Did I hate it? If so, why?" This idea of justifying a viewpoint with a reason is a big part of the self-evaluation process.

Students can keep self-reflections in a journal or notebook or these can be individual tasks done at the end of a slice of learning. Simple tasks like the formative assessment techniques in chapter 4 can be employed for self-reflective guides. Start with guides that offer basic reflective questions during the learning process:

For young learners, the reflection questions might be something like:

1. When you think about the lesson so far, what was the hardest part for you? Why?
2. What part of the lesson was easiest/most interesting to you? Why?

For older learners, the reflection questions might be more in depth:

1. Reflect on the lesson concepts so far. Which ones are easiest for you? Which are most difficult for you? Why?
2. What could you specifically do to support or extend your own understanding? For example, did your preparation, attention, or peer collaboration impact your understanding?
3. What could the teacher do to enhance your understanding? Please be specific.

## Self-Reflective Journal Writing

*Materials: Writing tools and a journal (See 5.5 mini hair band book directions on the book's companion website.)*

An age-old strategy for self-reflection and evaluation is journal writing. Remember that writing allows students to see their thoughts on paper. This process is especially helpful when self-assessing. Articulating thoughts on paper about your growth or areas for improvement is very useful in the learning development process.

There are a number of ways to use reflective journals. Some teachers like to have a journal for each content area. Another idea is to create a mini-journal that is used specifically to reflect on one project or task. The authors have used a unique mini-book for reflective writing that students of all ages find adaptive since additional pages can be added to the journal. The mini-book is created with a card stock cover, regular paper for the inside sheets, and a hair band to hold the book together. (See the directions for the hair band book, as well as links to bookmaking ideas, on our book's companion website.)

Note: There is an additional example of bookmaking and self-assessment on the book's companion website. See 5.6 elementary adjectives and adverbs book with self-assessment rubric. In addition, there is a website that is especially helpful called *Making Books*. You can locate this site online at http://makingbooks.com

## Self-Assessment Checklists and Rubrics

*Materials: Checklists and/or rubrics generated by the class and/or teacher or commercially created ones (See 5.7 oral presentation and self-assessment rubric and 5.8 generic self-assessment project rubric on the book's companion website.)*

The more specific guidelines a teacher can offer students, especially in the early stages of using self-assessment, the more meaningful the process will become. A teacher cannot simply say, "It's time now to self-assess your own work, have at it!" Without any guidelines for self-assessment, students are likely to self-assess by saying they did "Great," "Not so well," or they might even provide more colorful generic descriptions. Teachers should provide clear and specific guidelines for self-assessment. These specific measuring sticks can add clarity to the somewhat messy process students experience in identifying their own capabilities.

A note of caution: Be sure to give the criteria to the students before the start of the lesson or project in which students will be self-assessing. This will help them to focus on the specific criteria that are part of the learning goals. See figure 5.2 for an example of a self-assessment checklist for an oral presentation that would be appropriate for older learners.

*Conversational Self- and Peer Assessment*

One of the most engaging and active ways for students to self- or peer assess is through academic conversations to analyze either their own work or the work of others. The important elements in these discussions are clear and specific strategies for managing, implementing, and evaluating the conversations. Having techniques like self- or peer discussion prompts or specific criteria to evaluate will help make the process more valid and productive. A few conversational techniques are presented next.

*Critical Friends*

*Materials: These will vary based on the format of the process and the age of the students; criteria checklists or project rubrics would benefit this activity, as well as sample discussion questions*

The strategy of using *Critical Friends* to help students discuss, evaluate, and reflect on their learning progress and products is a technique that some teachers may already be using. In a helpful article on the topic written by Amy Reynolds (2009), she explains that "when students exchange feedback, the focus shifts from grades and competition to tangible aspects of a learner's work" (p. 55).

This experience of close examination of a peer's work and the resulting critical reflections can be a highly informative task. The bonus is that it takes away from the teacher some of the time-consuming process of giving detailed feedback to students. Further, students can truly take ownership of this authentic assessment method.

What does the Critical Friends process look like? From the authors' experiences, there are several situations where the use of this technique is highly effective. One way is for students to share with a peer or small group the

Student Name: _____

Date: _____

Presentation Topic: _____

| Category | Criteria | Comments |
|---|---|---|
| **Presentation Content** | I showed that I was well informed about the topic. | |
| | I used facts to back up the claims I made. | |
| | I remained focused on my main topic. | |
| | I engaged the audience and made the content interesting. | |
| | I was able to effectively answer questions about my topic at the end. | |
| **Delivery Techniques** | I kept eye contact with my audience. | |
| | I shared information in my own words rather than reading from slides or my notes. | |
| | I maintained a normal rate of speech, not too fast or too slow. | |
| | I used a voice that was clear and not too soft or too loud. | |
| | I used gestures in an effective way. | |
| **Organization** | My presentation had a clear beginning, middle, and end. | |
| | I let the audience know the purpose of my speech at the beginning. | |
| | My ideas flowed reasonably from one point to the next. | |
| **Presentation Aids/Resources** | The aids I used enhanced the presentation and didn't distract from the main focus. | |
| | I gave credit to the resources I used in my presentation. | |
| | The handouts and/or references were formatted correctly, with few or no errors. | |

Here's what I thought was the best thing about my presentation:

Here's what I would like to improve in a future presentation:

**Figure 5.2.  Oral presentation self-assessment checklist.**

final drafts of a culminating project or a writing assignment. Students will need rubrics or checklists of the assignment criteria handy to see if the work meets the expected learning outcomes. The idea is to share final drafts and discuss what elements are effective and what needs to be improved.

Students will benefit from having some conversation starters. For example, if middle-grade students are evaluating a science project on renewable energy, the teacher might have the rubric available but also provide open-ended prompts that promote a friendly yet critical conversation.

The student(s) evaluating the project might start by asking the project creator:

1. What did you like best about working on this project?
2. What part of the project was most challenging for you?

The peer evaluator(s) might then give feedback using the following guiding questions:

1. In reviewing the project, what are some things that are effective? Why?
2. In what ways did the project effectively demonstrate the renewable energy concepts our class has studied? Please be specific.
3. What types of specific suggestions do you have to improve the project?
4. Could you see this project as a realistic solution to renewable energy? Why?

The Critical Friends technique is a great way for students to learn how to articulate their views and cite reasons to support the feedback they are providing. In a collaborative classroom environment, students can have meaningful learning through the power of reflective and critical commentary. It's the teacher's job to help promote this climate and emphasize that the goal of the process is always on improvement and deeper learning.

*Line Up and Talk*

*Materials: Pre-made questions on slides or a chart; alternatively, have numbered questions on a handout to give students*

This is a good way to get students up from their seats and moving, as well as a quick way to add interest while reviewing and/or self-assessing lesson content. Start by having the students stand up and form two parallel lines so they are facing each other. Students will be talking with the person directly across from them. Have pre-made assessment questions about the lesson content to show or give the students.

Show the first question and prompt each pair of students to discuss how well they think they understand this component. After a minute or two, stop and call on students to share their responses to the question. Next, have only one line of students rotate one space so that each student discusses the next question with a new person.

A good way to add accountability or peer feedback is to have a handout that coordinates with the questions. Students can either self-assess or peer assess how well they could verbally explain their own level of understanding.

Alternatively, this strategy can be used as a warm-up discussion or a reading assignment conversation. This is a great activity to do outside, or if you are in a small room, students can form two shorter sets of lines. Finally, if you have an odd person who doesn't have a partner, let them be an observer and walk around and see which pairs are using good academic conversation strategies like taking turns talking and/or being active listeners.

## Examples of Conversation Prompts

Sometimes student academic conversations can be enhanced by giving sample prompts to students. This is especially helpful when students are just learning how to give feedback to each other. What follows are some examples of academic conversation prompts. The authors also highly recommend Jeff Zwiers's book *Academic Conversations* for a more in-depth look at this topic. The following are confirming prompts:

- Yes, that reminds me of . . .
- I see what you mean; it's kind of like . . .
- OK . . . so another example would be . . .

Here are reviewing prompts:

- So, what you're saying is . . .
- Is there anything else to add?
- I like the way you explained that . . .

And these are questioning prompts:

- What more could you say about . . .
- I'm not sure I understand?
- Can you explain it another way?

## FINAL THOUGHTS

Having students take ownership of assessment is a powerful yet controversial topic. Some will argue that students don't have the capacity to own or evaluate their own or their peers' learning. Other educators will embrace this concept and realize that self- and peer evaluation can provide deep and meaningful learning opportunities. The key is how the teacher frames it and how well the process is planned and taught to students.

Keep in mind that teachers can benefit from self- and peer assessment as well. Try tape recording a future lesson and then reflect on the effectiveness of the instruction. Alternatively, try to arrange for a colleague to observe a teaching strategy and provide feedback. Teachers need critical friends as well!

## POST-READING QUESTIONS

1. What is the value in having students self-assess their own learning?
2. What student dispositions are helpful for effective self-assessment?
3. How can you create learning environments conducive to student ownership of assessment?
4. What are some of the challenges and benefits of peer assessment?
5. How can you add depth and variety to self- or peer assessments?

## POST-READING QUESTIONS WITH AUTHOR COMMENTARY

**What is the value in having students self-assess their own learning?** In this chapter, we have presented the case for student ownership of learning. Teachers must come to realize that in the final analysis, they cannot force students to learn. Students need to be shown that they play a huge role in the attainment of knowledge and skills. When students clearly understand learning goals and how to determine if those goals have been met, they can more effectively begin the self-assessment process. Of course, all of this takes time, effort, careful planning, modeling, and implementing. We strongly believe that these efforts are well worth it.

**What student dispositions are helpful for effective self-assessment?** Many times, students enter the learning process unaware of the value of self-assessment or how their own personal dispositions can either enhance or detract from the process. This is where it is helpful for teachers to discuss, model, and provide opportunities for students to develop some of the qualities that promote self-evaluative thinking and actions.

The qualities we have covered in this chapter included intrinsic motivation, autonomy, metacognitive thinking, and resilience. We believe that when these traits are explicitly promoted and nurtured, students' abilities to successfully self-evaluate can be vastly improved.

**How can you create learning environments conducive to student ownership of assessment?** Educators must be intentional when designing and implementing experiences that involve self- or peer-assessment strategies.

The process should be scaffolded, just like a teacher would gradually introduce the elements of a new skill. First, students must have a clear understanding of the learning goals and the criteria of the assessment. Next, they need to know what good self- or peer assessing looks like.

Additionally, students need a variety of self- or peer-assessment strategies that can be customized to meet the needs of various student populations. Finally, there should be some sort of feedback about the process and ways that students can move forward to their next steps in reaching deeper and more meaningful ways to own their learning.

**What are some of the challenges and benefits of peer assessment?** Based on our experiences with students, peer assessment can either be a valuable learning situation or an unproductive use of instructional time. It seems to depend on the way peer assessment is framed and modeled for students. We have found that when peer assessment is presented and managed effectively, it can be a very valuable learning tool. Most students like to choose their own peer assessor. Usually they pick another student they know and feel comfortable sharing work with.

Younger students will need lots of modeling and even a checklist or set of a few specific criteria to help structure the conversations. Older students will be more ready to justify feedback and get into deeper nuances about the topics. In any event, it is extremely helpful if the teacher gathers feedback from the students after a peer-review activity. We have found it extremely helpful to find out directly from our students what went well and what might be improved for a future peer-assessment task. Students can evaluate your process or they can self-assess the quality of their own participation.

**How can you add depth and variety to self- or peer assessments?** As with most instruction, occasionally it's a good idea to add some variation to the method and the complexity of the task. Of course, when first implementing self- or peer assessment, we suggest to start slow, adding in lots of modeling and examples. Most teachers begin with rudimentary elements of the task, such as self- or peer assessing a less complex task, and then gradually increasing the depth of the criteria for the assessment.

Remember that students can't evaluate something when they don't have an idea of what "good" looks like. We have used checklists with specific criteria or rubrics to guide students during the self- or peer-assessment experience. We also believe it is critical to talk to students about the value of specific feedback.

For example, if students are assessing a peer and they just respond with comments like "good job" or "try harder," that type of feedback is not very helpful. Instead, we suggest that you provide prompts like those for the Critical Friends discussion to guide students toward giving more explicit feedback.

We have tried numerous unique ways to spice up the peer-assessment process, including going outside and having peers find a quiet spot to talk and reflect on their work. Other times students might peer-assess class presentations or projects prepared by classmates. Again, having short feedback forms with a checklist or comment section is helpful. We have found that positive comments and constructive suggestions can be offered and accepted by most students if a class climate is built on mutual respect and a desire to improve.

## CHAPTER NOTES ON SELF-DETERMINATION THEORY

Self-determination theory (SDT) is a theory of motivation. It is concerned with supporting humans' natural or intrinsic leanings to behave in effective and healthy ways. The theory was originally advanced by Edward Deci and Richard Ryan and has been researched, elaborated, and refined by scholars from around the world.

A component of SDT focuses on how social and cultural factors can add or detract from a person's sense of personal volition and initiative. Conditions supporting the individual's experience of *autonomy*, *competence*, and *relatedness* are argued to nurture the most volitional and high levels of motivation. In addition, SDT proposes that to the degree to which any of these three psychological needs is unsupported within a social context there can be a detrimental impact on wellness in that setting (Ryan & Deci, 2000).

Self-determination has strong implications for classroom practice. Extensive research based on SDT suggests that both intrinsic motivation and autonomous types of extrinsic motivation are conducive to engagement and learning in educational contexts (Niemiec & Ryan, 2009). Evidence also suggests that teachers' support of students' basic psychological needs for autonomy, competence, and relatedness facilitates students' self-regulation for learning, academic performance, and well-being.

Johnmarshall Reeve (2006) has done extensive work on helping teachers know how they can help foster autonomous behavior in educational settings. He has identified ways to better motivate students to learn at all educational levels. Through his extensive research, he has found that teachers can learn strategies that promote student autonomy and well-being.

Strategies for enhancing autonomy include providing choice and meaningful rationales for learning activities, acknowledging students' feelings about those topics, and minimizing pressure and control. Strategies for enhancing competence include providing specific feedback and challenging tasks. Strategies for enhancing relatedness include conveying warmth, caring, and respect to students (Niemiec & Ryan, 2009).

The bottom line is that when students are shown that they have the capacity for competence and can have ownership of their learning, powerful knowledge-forming experiences can happen.

## REFERENCES

Brookhart, S., Moss, C., & Long, B. (2008). Formative assessment that empowers. *Educational Leadership, 66*(3), 52–57.

Condly, S. J. (2006). Resilience in children: A review of literature with implications for education. *Urban Education, 41*(3), 211–236.

Deci, E. L., Vallerand, R. J., Pelletier, L. G., & Ryan, R. M. (1991). Motivation and education: The self-determination perspective. *Educational Psychologist, 26*(3), 325–346.

Kohn, A. (1999). *Punished by rewards: The trouble with gold stars, incentive plans, As, praise, and other bribes.* New York: Houghton Mifflin.

Niemiec, C. P., & Ryan M. R. (2009). Autonomy, competence, and relatedness in the classroom: Applying self-determination theory to educational practice. *Theory and Research in Education, 7*(2), 133–144.

Reeve, J. (2006). Teachers as facilitators: What autonomy-supportive teachers do and why their students benefit. *The Elementary School Journal, 106*(3), 225–236.

Reynolds, A. (2009). Why every student needs critical friends. *Educational Leadership, 76*(3), 54–57.

Ryan, R. M., & Deci, E. L. (2000). Self-determination theory and the facilitation of intrinsic motivation, social development, and well-being. *American Psychologist, 55,* 68–78.

Ryan, R. M., & Deci, E. L. (2017). *Self-determination theory: Basic psychological needs in motivation, development, and wellness.* New York: Guilford Press.

Sebba, J., Crick, R. D., Yu, G., Lawson, H., Harlen, W., & Durant, K. (2008). Systematic review of research evidence of the impact on students in secondary schools of self and peer assessment. *Research Evidence in Education Library series.* London: EPPI-Centre. Social Science Research Unit, Institute of Education, University of London. Retrieved from http:// eppi. ioe. ac. uk/cms/Default. aspx

Taylor, G., Jungert, T., Mageau, G. A., Schattke, K., Dedic, H., Rosenfield, S., & Koestner, R. (2014). A self-determination theory approach to predicting school achievement over time: The unique role of intrinsic motivation. *Contemporary Educational Psychology, 39*(4), 342–358.

Zwiers, J. (2011). *Academic conversations: Classroom talk that fosters critical thinking and content understandings.* Portland, ME: Stenhouse Publishers.

*Chapter Six*

# Solution Four

*Implement 21st-Century Assessment*

"Know what's weird? Day by day, nothing seems to change, but pretty soon . . . everything's different."—Calvin from *Calvin and Hobbes* by Bill Watterson

## PRE-READING QUESTIONS

Before reading this chapter, it may be helpful to consider your prior knowledge and/or opinions regarding the following questions:

1. How can assessment be responsive to the instructional needs of 21st-century learners?
2. What underlying beliefs about teaching and learning promote a forward-thinking approach to the design and implementation of assessment strategies?
3. What types of assignments and assessments best measure and promote the skills needed for learners of the future?
4. How can educators embrace and utilize technological tools to enhance 21st-century teaching and learning?
5. What can educators do to promote the implementation of 21st-century assignments and assessments?

After completing this chapter, you can revisit these questions and review some final commentary from the authors. See the section Post-Reading Questions near the end of the chapter.

## INTRODUCTION

Evidence abounds that there are vast changes in the types of knowledge, skills, and experiences that students need for their future world of work and life. One significant change includes the removal of geographical barriers that once perpetuated the seclusion and isolation of various regions and cultures. Current illustrative quips include phrases such as: the world is not as large as it used to be, society is becoming a cultural melting pot, or schools must work on increasing academic rigor in order to prepare students to compete within the global marketplace. This newfound geographical proximity has resulted largely from advances in technology. Because of these advances, regions and cultures that were traditionally removed from exploration are now easily accessible and currently included in global policy considerations, qualitative and quantitative research literature, and P–12 classroom discussions.

The advent of global consciousness and an abundance of novel technologies have resulted in increasing challenges for educators. Among these challenges are pressing concerns about what 21st-century curriculum, instruction, and assessment should look like. Many wonder if their educational systems have already reached the point where the current means and methods of assessment are too outdated to measure the abilities required for 21st-century learners.

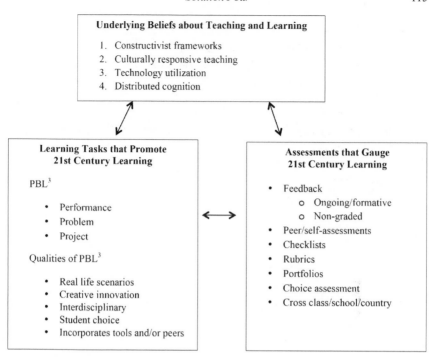

**Figure 6.1.  Elements that contribute to teachers' success with 21st-century assessment.**

## MODELS THAT GUIDE EFFECTIVE TEACHER AND STUDENT SUCCESS WITH 21ST-CENTURY ASSESSMENT

In order to understand futuristic approaches to assessment, it is necessary to first possess an awareness of what 21st-century teachers and students need in order to thrive. Teachers in contemporary classrooms will need to know how to effectively facilitate, engage, and inspire students in using these modern approaches to education and the assessment of that learning. Likewise, students will need additional competencies that schools have not traditionally used to teach and assess.

In this chapter, two central models guide the concepts presented to make school assessments more relevant for today's learners. These models were created after much research and literature review, and more importantly from input gathered from students, teachers, and instructional leaders. Figure 6.1 displays the factors that make up the assessment proficiencies essential for 21st-century teachers (i.e., pedagogical beliefs and values, instructional approaches, and assessment applications), and figure 6.2 shows six factors contributing to students' success with 21st-century assessments (i.e., being self-aware, constructive, critically reflective, collaborative, technologically competent, and globally and culturally responsive).

Before discussing each model with specificity, it should be understood that although these beliefs and competencies represent best practices to engender 21st-century learning, they in no way represent the gamut of underlying beliefs or competencies required, nor do they replace those peripheral teaching philosophies and pedagogies that educators hold in high regard and find utility in practicing.

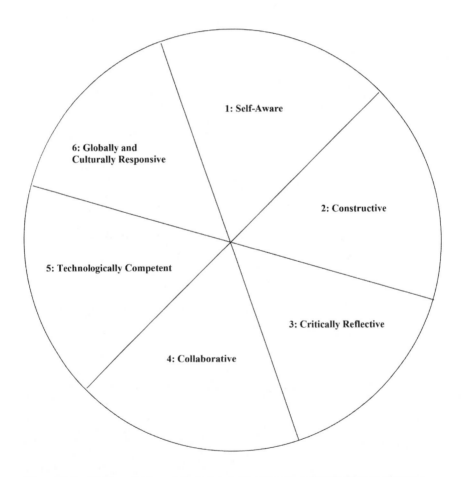

Figure 6.2.   Factors that contribute to students' success with 21st-century assessments.

# ELEMENTS THAT CONTRIBUTE TO A TEACHER'S SUCCESS WITH 21ST-CENTURY ASSESSMENT: UNDERLYING BELIEFS ABOUT TEACHING AND LEARNING

Many theories abound within the research and pedagogical literature about which instructional approaches prove most beneficial for developing the content, learning, and cognitive capabilities of 21st-century students. Twenty-first-century skills often require students to demonstrate mastery through performances and products.

Therefore, due to the applied nature of the 21st-century skills, the more pervasive and applicable theories and practices are those instructional strategies and assessment design principles that (1) embed the constructivist framework, (2) are culturally responsive, (3) utilize technological tools, and (4) maximize the benefits of distributed cognition. The next section will take a closer look at how educators endorse each of these four elements to aid in the teaching, learning, and assessment of 21st-century competencies.

## Element 1: Embedding Constructivist Frameworks

Simply put, constructivism is not so much about the instructional approach to learning as it is about *the way* in which students conceptualize and internalize content. Constructivism has been influenced by an impressive lineage of great educational thinkers and researchers such as John Dewey, Jean Piaget, and Lev Vygotsky. According to Schunk (2012), constructivism assumes that people are *active* learners and that they will develop knowledge for themselves—regardless of what an educator may intend throughout the learning cycle.

Because of this inherent tendency for learners to construct their own meaning from instruction, as well as from their interaction with the content itself, it is imperative that teachers provide students with the opportunity to make connections by discovering the basic principles within a concept. If not allowed this opportunity, students' abilities to engage in and mobilize self-directed learning through discovery will be significantly reduced—as will be the likelihood of educators ever facilitating constructivist-oriented classrooms with fidelity.

Pragmatically, constructivism represents a departure from the traditional, teacher-centered form of teaching and learning and, in effect, acts as the predominant theory underpinning both student-centered learning and integrated curricula efforts. It is assumed that persons, behaviors, and environments are interdependent and connected. In this environment, teachers typically avoid presenting concepts as isolated pieces. Instead, there is a constant examination of how discrete ideas, skills, and procedures fit together to form larger understandings.

Although there are variations in the range of approaches to constructivist teaching, a common attribute characteristic to all constructivist teaching is that learners engaged in constructivist classrooms are "actively involved with content through manipulation of materials and social interaction" (Schunk, 2012, p. 231). Therefore, students in constructivist classrooms often touch, see, talk about, manipulate, question, and collaboratively interact with the content (and its tools) in their efforts to construct meaning and to actually *learn*.

The teacher's role within the constructivist classroom is to act as a facilitator of students' constructed knowledge. Depending on the stage of concept acquisition, the constructivist-minded teacher chooses appropriate instructional strategies, curriculum materials, and classroom support systems to provide for varying learner needs. When exposing students to new skills the teacher uses models, explanations, visuals, and real-life scenarios to bring new content to life for students.

In the practice stage of learning, the teacher constantly scaffolds opportunities for students to try out new tasks and gives an abundance of feedback so students can learn from mistakes. In the application stage of learning, the teacher is on standby, waiting to pose challenging, remediating, or extension questions that will further clarify and develop students' content-level knowledge and proficiency.

If teachers are interested in creating constructivist classrooms grounded in students' intrinsically and self-regulated work with meaningful tasks, Brooks and Brooks (1999) have offered five, easy-to-implement, guiding principles by which to facilitate the constructivist environment. These principles are:

1. Pose problems of emerging relevance to students in which teachers situate the academic content and standards within the context of students' actual lives.
2. Structure learning around overarching concepts via the quest for *essence*—thinking about the enduring understandings that the students need to know, understand, and be able to do.
3. Seek and value students' points of view by providing an opportunity for students to share their unique perspectives.
4. Adapt curriculum to address students' suppositions. Once students voice their perspectives, validate those perspectives by integrating them within future problems, situations, conversations, and the like.
5. Assess student learning in the context of teaching. When assessing, look at it from the standpoint of "Where am I going next?" instead of "What do my students *still* not know?" (Brooks & Brooks, 1999, pp. 35–85).

Each of these guiding principles contributes not only to student engagement and social interaction but also to culturally responsive instruction and assessment, as each of these guiding principles is primarily focused on building students' sense of efficacy, agency, and self.

Finally, there can be strong elements of constructivist thinking in the design and implementation of classroom assessments. The idea of students having a personal buy-in to the instructional process cannot be more clearly seen than in student self- and peer assessment. More on this topic of student ownership was detailed in chapter 5.

## Element 2: Being Culturally Responsive

In our multicultural society, it is essential for teachers to understand, embrace, and exhibit constructive behavior about people of all cultures. Culture plays a role not only in communication but also in the thinking, learning, and assessment processes that happen in school settings. According to Gloria Ladson-Billings (1994), culturally responsive teaching is a pedagogy that recognizes the importance of including students' cultural orientations in all aspects of learning.

Teachers who embrace culturally responsive pedagogy exhibit the factors necessary for 21st-century learning experiences. One imperative factor is that the teacher exhibit positive perspectives on students, parents, and the community in conjunction with communication of high expectations. Learning experiences can also be connected to the context of the community culture and support the relevance of learning to real-life scenarios.

From a theoretical perspective, culturally responsive teaching is aligned with *critical pedagogy*. Critical pedagogy is an axiological, or *value-focused*, philosophy that emphasizes the need for educators to provide outlets for students to voice their perspectives—and to have those perspectives validated. Pioneered by Paulo Freire, critical pedagogy is a concept that teaches teachers and their students to perform three tasks: (a) "to name, (b) to critically reflect, and (c) to act" (Freire, 1970/2000; Wink, 2011, p. 46).

According to Freire, the *naming* aspect of this paradigm requires both the teacher and the student to identify, or *name*, their varied perspectives in light of, or in contrast to, the overriding perspective. Fortunately, many opportunities exist within multicultural classrooms for students to articulate alternative perspectives. Example topics include religion, class dichotomies, gender roles, civil rights, or any other narratives relevant to the cultural or societal concerns that earmark the composition of the classroom.

The purpose of *naming* one's perspective is to place, within the forefront of everyone's mind, an awareness of the position, challenges, or acts of marginalization that affect a particular group. These topics can effectively be

merged into assignments and their accompanying assessments through strategies such as Socratic dialogues, debates, or problem-solving tasks.

The *critically reflective* component of critical pedagogy requires teachers
and students to consider how their unique perspectives relate to, confirm,
impede, or extend their own and the group's dialogue regarding the topic of
discussion. It allows students to understand how their own experiences and
sense of self fit within the context of the learning environment and the social
world. It also allows students to see how their preconceived notions and
resulting verbal and nonverbal responses affect the notions and behaviors of
those around them.

This critically reflective dialogue also enables students to consider and
conceptualize how their actions could operate to validate, alleviate, or alto-
gether remove restrictive and inhibitory practices or habits of mind (i.e.,
prejudices).

The culmination of critical pedagogy lies within the final step—the call
for *action*. The *action* domain of critical pedagogy requires those engaged in
the conversation to consider and mobilize ways in which to eradicate social
structures and systems that serve to perpetuate prejudices and inequities.

After unveiling what was once hidden, dialoguing about and determining
a plan of action, and finally following through with that plan of action to
engender more culturally and critically responsive classrooms, teachers will
enjoy the successes that come with empowering students to be self-aware yet
globally responsive.

Culturally responsive teaching, like constructivist approaches to instruction, thrives on social interaction and contextually relevant classroom tasks
and assessments. So the answer for the educator trying to respond to the
required technological competencies in contemporary classrooms is to make
the academic content *contextually relevant* and conceptually whole. The only
other question in preparing 21st-century learners for the competencies required of them so that they can be successful in their future roles is: How can
learning and assessment in the technological era be both constructivist and
culturally responsive?

Fortunately, there are a number of technological tools that can help teachers meet the demands of 21st-century learners, while also being responsive to
students' unique learning styles and cultural backgrounds. The utilization of
these tools will be discussed next.

## Element 3: Utilizing Technological Tools

No discussion of 21st-century learning would be complete without mention
of the impact of technological tools and social media. Innovations and rapid
changes in communication and access to information seem to be increasing
exponentially each year. Educators have to play catch up in order to keep

abreast of the sweeping changes in teaching and learning due to advances in technology.

In chapter 4, several examples of interactive web tools were mentioned as solutions to gather data and give feedback for the purpose of informative assessment. In this chapter, a broader set of tools and links is offered. All the updated links and resources are available on the book's companion website noted in the front of this book.

Tables 6.1 and 6.2 provide an assortment of current technological resources, which have been codified by colleagues Jeff Hall and Lucy Bush (see www.mathedtech.pbworks.com). This resource provides an extensive depository of novel applications, constructivist approaches to problem solving, and lists of additional technological advancements. Although the content area focus of the site is mathematics, the salience of each tool's utility proves beneficial to share with teachers of all content areas and across interdisciplinary fields of study.

**Table 6.1.  21st-Century Technological Tools**

| Domain | Site Name | Utility |
| --- | --- | --- |
| 3D Software | 3DTin | Graphics Modeling |
| | Google SketchUp | |
| Online Education Assistance | Academic Earth | Videos, Lectures, Courses |
| | AdaptedMind | Adaptive Learning for Grades 1–6 |
| | Better Explained | Intuitive Explanations |
| | CK–12 | Textbooks (free) |
| | Coursera | |
| | Dreambox | Adaptive Lessons for K–8 |
| | e-booksdirectory | Textbooks (free) |
| | Go2Web2.0 | Index of E-Learning Tools |
| | Mathspace | Adaptive Problems and Guided Feedback |
| | MobyMax | CCSS-Based Adaptive Lessons |
| | SchoolYourself | Interactive Math Lessons |
| Animation and Videos | Animoto | |
| | Factorization | |
| | Go!Animate | Create Your Own Cartoons |

|                                      |                              |                                                          |
|--------------------------------------|------------------------------|----------------------------------------------------------|
|                                      | Mathematics Animated         | QuickTime Animations                                     |
|                                      | PowToon                      |                                                          |
|                                      | Russell Kightley Media       | Science and Math Animations                              |
| Interactive Whiteboard Resources     | Cool Timer                   | Countdown Timer                                          |
|                                      | Desmos                       | Graphing Calculator                                      |
|                                      | Explain Everything           | Turns iPads into Interactive Whiteboards                 |
|                                      | Hoodamath                    | Games                                                    |
|                                      | Learning Can Be Fun          | Links to Sites and Activities                            |
|                                      | Max's Math Adventures        | Word Problems                                            |
|                                      | PhET Interactive             | Science Simulations                                      |
|                                      | Promethean Planet            |                                                          |
| STEM and Robotics                    | Carnegie Mellon              |                                                          |
|                                      | DUST                         | Augmented Reality                                        |
|                                      | Future City                  |                                                          |
|                                      | NASA Stem Challenges         | Grades 5–8                                               |
|                                      | Robotics Academy             |                                                          |
|                                      | Robot Algebra                |                                                          |
|                                      | Robot Events                 |                                                          |
|                                      | TEAMS                        | Tests of Engineering Aptitude, Mathematics, and Science  |
| Problem Solving                      | Art of Problem Solving       |                                                          |
|                                      | Max's Math Adventures        |                                                          |
|                                      | Problem Solving Decks for K–8 |                                                         |
|                                      | Word Problem Resources Online |                                                         |
|                                      | ProjectSOLVE                 |                                                          |
| Interdisciplinary                    | GeoMath                      | Geography and Mathematics                                |
|                                      | Living Math                  | Resources for Holistic Mathematics Instruction           |

| | STEM Georgia | Cross-Disciplinary Links and Resources |
| | ZooTech | Astronomy and Mathematics |

**Table 6.2. PBL3 Assessment Technologies**

| Domain | Website Name | Utility |
| --- | --- | --- |
| General Assessments | ClassFlow | Interactive Lessons and Assessments |
| | Formative | Real-Time Assessments (Including Drawings) |
| | Google Classroom | |
| | GoSoapBox | |
| | Haiku Learning | |
| | Kickboard | |
| | Mentimeter | |
| | NearPod | |
| | Nutmeg | CCSS-Based Assessments and Analyses |
| | Office Mix | PowerPoint Presentations and Assessments |
| | TestMoz | |
| | That Quiz | Mini-Assessments |
| Easy Grading | InstaGrade | Scan Quizzes with iPhone |
| | ZipGrade | Scan Quizzes with Apple/ Android Phone or Tablet |
| Review Games | Braingenie | Self-Quizzes and Multiplayer Matches |
| | Kahoot! | Game Show Style |
| | FlipQuiz | Game Show Style Quiz Boards |
| | BrainRush | Adaptive Learning Games |
| | Math Games | |
| | Quizlet | Flashcards and Study Games |
| | Quizizz | Multiplayer Quiz Games |
| | Geometry Jeopardy | |
| | JeopardyLabs | Build or Browse |

|  | Permutation | |
|---|---|---|
|  | Combination Jeopardy | |
|  | PowerPoint: Wheel of Fortune | |
|  | Who Wants to Be a Millionaire? | Math Game |
| Student Response Systems | ClassPager | |
|  | ExitTicket | |
|  | Infuse Learning | |
|  | Plickers | |
|  | Poll Everywhere | |
|  | Survey Monkey | |
| Quiz and Test Generators | Problem Attic | |
|  | ProProfs | Create Quizzes, Games, etc. |
|  | QuizPop | |
|  | Socrative | |
|  | QuizStar | |
| Video and Quiz Embedding Resources | Blubbr | Create Video Trivia Games |
|  | EDpuzzle | Embed Quizzes in Videos |
|  | eduCanon | Add Assessments to Videos |
|  | FlipGrid | Respond via Recorded Videos |
|  | Grade Cam | Grade Assessments with a Camera |
|  | Zaption | Add Questions to Online Videos |
| Storage and Portfolios | FreshGrade | Digital Portfolios |
|  | Dropbox | Multipurpose Storage |
|  | Google Drive | |
|  | iCloud | |
|  | Minus | |
|  | SkyDrive | |

| International Resources | Japanese National Assessment | 6th- and 9th-Grade Math Problems |
| --- | --- | --- |
| | Singapore Math | Placement Tests |
| | Dreambox | Lesson and Assessment Samples |
| | Khan Academy | Videos and Practice Problems |

## Element 4: Maximizing the Benefits of Distributed Cognition

Because of the vast quantity of technological tools available for educators, it's important for teachers to consider a different approach to the way they interpret the function of these tools for day-to-day usage. Educators must keep in mind that they are not preparing students just for tomorrow or a few years from now. Glimpses of the world of work for future generations are a difficult vision to imagine, but teachers must realize that they don't have a choice. They must, for the sake of students, provide instruction that gives learners opportunities to understand and utilize technological tools.

Instructors will need more concrete models of ways to design complex learning that can simulate the 21st-century world of work where tools, minds, and environments create communities of distributed knowledge that would not be possible in solitary situations. To help understand how tools can actually be a part of a student's brainpower, the concept of distributed cognition needs to be understood.

Think about the cell phone, for example. Most people accept this *smart* device as a means for storing data that would otherwise be stored in their brains. People don't waste mind space or energy trying to remember phone numbers, addresses, or rote information because they can instantly access this data with their cell phones. Imagine if teachers embraced this concept and allowed students to use tools and peers as an extension of their cognitive capabilities.

In 1995, Edwin Hutchins was the first to systematically detail the cognitive elements of distributed cognition in his book *Cognition in the Wild*. Hutchins arrived at his conclusions through detailed notes and observations during a study of how navigating a ship is accomplished through the collaborative effects of the crewmembers and their interactions with one another and the tools on the vessel. Hutchins found that collectively, rather than individually, through shared interactions with multiple artifacts and technologies, a community of knowledge was formed that successfully completed the navigation tasks.

As in the previous example, in a distributed cognition system, tools and other individuals are considered equivalent active participants. This type of cognition occurs when one cognitive task (e.g., critical analysis) is distributed among individuals and tools so that no one person is required to complete the overall task. The cognition that is represented by the system is greater than the sum of its parts.

On a regular basis, humans rely on a vast host of artifacts to help make sense of their world. Today, there are calculators and spreadsheets for quick and easy mathematical calculations, speech synthesizers and word processors to process and refine verbal and written communication, and GPS and other electronic mapping tools to support navigation. How much of your cognitive energy and capability is distributed among tools such as these?

In 1993, Roy Pea proposed the idea that "tools literally carry intelligence *in* them" (p. 53) in that they can represent something that can be conceived of as a carrier of human patterns of reasoning. In all types of settings, and particularly the educational setting, how often is an artifact given credit for the *intelligence* residing in a tool? One glaring exception is the ban of calculators from many school testing scenarios. However, modern tools and electronics, such as the electronic thesaurus or cell phone, are so ubiquitous that they almost become invisible as cognitive dimensions.

Can it be that educators are not fully cognizant of the distributed cognitive effect from the usage of tools? Educators embrace the idea of scaffolds for learning, but how often are technology tools seen as scaffolds for cognition? Technological tools can make cognitive tasks easier or more efficient, and in some instances, they provide a means of accomplishing cognitive tasks that could not be performed without the tools. Recognizing cognitive support of technology tools is a crucial element that will need to be shown to educators in the design of instructional tasks and the accompanying assessments (Carr, Johnson, & Bush, 2016).

In thinking about 21st-century assignments and assessments, teachers will need to consider the role of distributed cognition. Learning tasks and the assessment of these tasks will have to be redesigned to allow for more tool and peer utilization. Information that can be *googled* in a few seconds might not need to be assessed. What will need to be measured is the way information is collected, critically analyzed, and applied to a vast array of situations.

## FACTORS THAT CONTRIBUTE TO STUDENTS' SUCCESS WITH 21ST-CENTURY ASSESSMENTS

Beyond changes in the curriculum content, there are a myriad of competencies that students will need to possess in order to be successful. These factors also complement several of the capabilities outlined by Partnership for 21st-Century Schools (see more about their model at the end of chapter notes). The next section will briefly describe, or review as applicable, what teachers can do to help cultivate the 21st-century student competencies identified in figure 6.2.

## Factor I: Self-Awareness

The first trait that is a contributing factor of 21st-century learners' success is an awareness of self. This awareness of self subsists as students' knowledge and personal appraisals of their academic, behavior, and social skills. In chapters 3, 4, 5, and at the beginning of chapter 6, the importance of students' ownership of learning and assessment is discussed. These chapters offer an array of strategies through which teachers can facilitate student ownership (i.e., data dialogues, reflective journal writing, self-regulated learning and assessment, and constructivist pedagogy).

It is important to point out that becoming self-aware starts as a critically reflective process that is constructed via students' analyses of their own processes and products. Over time, students can more readily identify and know how to best develop their strengths and seek support for areas of weakness. The 21st-century learner's sense of self-awareness is a competency that is essential to and precedes all others.

## Factor II: Knowledge Construction

The second characteristic required of 21st-century students is the ability to construct meaning. As previously described within this chapter, students can develop their own knowledge through opportunities to explore, watch others, experiment, make mistakes, and apply small pieces of learning to build big ideas. Similarly, this happens when students are given time and space to interpret and internalize information based on their own knowledge, previous experiences, and interactions with the social world.

As a reminder, constructivist teaching and learning enables students to engage in the self-regulatory actions of being self-directed, self-monitoring, and self-assessing—all of which are skills needed in order for students to be able to solve global problems. Later in the chapter, the constructivist approaches to teaching and assessment that are specifically aimed toward building constructive and self-regulated habits of mind will be examined.

## Factor III: Critical Reflection

Another key student attribute is the ability to be critically reflective. At the beginning of the chapter, the concept and practice of *critical reflection*—the act of identifying, situating, and resolving differing beliefs and systems within multiple environments—was explored. It is this practice of and ability to critically reflect that can distinguish competent 21st-century learners. Due to the inherent interconnectedness of global markets, technologies, and conflicts, 21st-century students must possess a greater sense of awareness and responsibility if society is to continue to effectively collaborate and advance.

For many teachers, giving students time to reflect seems an unwarranted or unnecessary use of instructional time. However, researchers such as Cleary and Zimmerman (2004) have found significant improvements in student learning from the use of student reflection and self-regulation. When students are shown the steps in the reflection process, how to critically reflect and set goals for improvement, amazing results can happen.

For an excellent review of the process of student reflection and numerous strategies for teaching students how to go about self-reflection, refer to the book *Learning and Leading with Habits of Mind* (2008) by Arthur Costa and Bena Kallick.

## Factor IV: Collaboration

Collaboration in the 21st century is more than working in groups to design and showcase a product. Collaboration in the 21st century consists of hearing and embracing alternative approaches and perspectives to problem solving. In its essence, it is students' ability to move beyond the "tried and true" perspective, to successfully hear, accommodate, and actively pursue a novel or divergent approach of finding resolution. The ability to collaborate represents a synergy of critical thinking and reflective capacity as students must identify and move beyond what they know in order to reach consensus and complete the objective.

Teachers realize through the work of Vygotsky and others that students learn through social interaction. However, knowing how to effectively incorporate academic conversations is another thing. Collaborative learning has become such a buzzword in educational arenas that many times teachers just have students form pairs and tell them to talk about a topic. This can often end up with students having casual conversations that have nothing to do with the content being studied. Teachers must take collaborative learning seriously. They need to offer ways to model, organize, and add accountability factors into collaborative work.

In chapters 4 and 5, numerous strategies are given that offer concrete ways for teachers to promote the effective use of collaborative learning. Some of the best strategy structures for cooperative learning are those generated by Spencer Kagan. See his website https://www.kaganonline.com/ for a wealth of resources to enhance collaborative student interactions.

## Factor V: Technological Competentence

Most students automatically embrace technology, especially in social settings. However, do students really have the technological savvy to be successful citizens of the 21st century? In a 2016 study conducted by Sherah Carr, along with her colleagues Nneka Johnson and Lucy Bush, teachers reported that "students lacked the technology savvy to adequately use the tools to reach the more complex capabilities that generate problem solving and deeper thinking" (p.171).

While the students were competent with social media tools like Twitter, Facebook, or Snapchat, they were unsure of how to effectively utilize tools like spreadsheets or multimedia applications. Furthermore, when it came to critically analyzing information gathered from online sources, students could be easily convinced by undocumented information.

What these examples exemplify is that students may demonstrate no fear of technology or have surface-level social skills with various applications. However, there remains a need for deeper and more precise experiences for students. These needs include having the time, the models, and the training to effectively use technology to solve complex problems and communicate powerful ideas.

## Factor VI: Global and Cultural Responsiveness

Global and cultural responsiveness represents the culmination of the five factors previously outlined. If students are able to (a) be self-aware, (b) construct meaning from data, (c) be critically reflective, (d) see the value of and engage in collaboration, and (e) know how to effectively use technology, they will be well equipped for the future. These kinds of skills also encourage personal responsibility and resilience in young people, so they can thoughtfully respond to an array of global and cultural issues, problems, and conflicts that come about as novel technologies evolve.

However, more important, within this competency resides the intention and the hope that the current work of stakeholders and educators has imparted a positive effect on the future. When this collective group provides sufficient and appropriate responses to students' needs, in preparation for their futures, 21st-century learners will not only improve the economy, intergroup relations, and the environment, but they will also impart these competencies into the generations of learners that follow them.

## LEARNING TASKS AND ASSESSMENTS THAT PROMOTE 21ST-CENTURY LEARNING

### PBL[3] Overview

Earlier in the chapter, the authors described teacher beliefs that operate to facilitate students' acquisition of 21st-century competencies. Those principles included embedding constructivism, being culturally responsive, utilizing technology, and maximizing the benefits of distributed cognition.

However, beyond these beliefs there is the larger challenge for educators of designing learning tasks and assessments that match the needs of 21st-century learners. It's one thing for a teacher to read and theorize about how to teach in a manner conducive to constructivist teaching and learning. Knowing how to operationalize these ideas is another matter. In the next few sections of the chapter, you will be provided a cursory analysis of three models of constructivist teaching: problem-based, project-based, and performance-based learning and assessment (see PBL[3]; figure 6.3).

## What Is Problem-Based Learning?

Problem-based learning is a student-centered instructional strategy that facilitates students' learning of subject matter within the context of an authentic, *ill-structured* problem (Stanford University, 2001). In problem-based learning, the class works together to identify a problem or question that has personal significance.

The problem can be students' self-identified problems, current debates within a content domain or field of study, or can be based on an assessment item that students demonstrated difficulty with answering. Whatever the identified problem, the key to problem development resides within ensuring

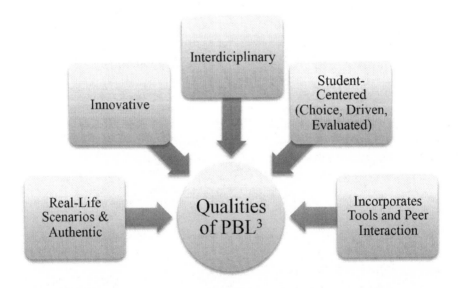

**Figure 6.3. Shared features of problem-based, project-based, and performance-based learning (PBL[3]).**

the presence of the following attributes (Stanford University, 2001). The problem must:

1. Generate interest, controversy, and investment.
2. Contain multiple solution paths.
3. Require more information in order to resolve it.
4. Be malleable (e.g., can change as needed, does not operationally prefer one method of problem solving over another, is open-ended in the interpretation and resolution).

Following development of the problem (whether predetermined by the teacher or created by the students), the role of the teacher is to serve as an instructional resource. During this segment of problem-based learning, the teacher provides the content materials, multimedia resources, or brainstorming tools that would best serve to inspire students' design and implementation of a resolution to the problem.

Once students are equipped with the tools necessary to solve the problem, the actual work of problem-based learning begins—for the students, that is. Throughout the learning cycle, students self-identify and explore what they already know about the topic and then use that background knowledge to determine what they need to know in order to reach and present a solution.

Students subsequently engage in management and leadership roles—deciding intermediate tasks and the person responsible, collaborating via iterative forms of written and verbal communication, and employing reasoning and critical-thinking capabilities to arrive at a conclusion. After students decide on the appropriateness of their final response, each team or group of students articulates their findings via reports or other forms of presentation to the whole class. The whole class then engages in assessment of each group's solutions—determining among themselves the more efficient strategies and appropriate responses to the problem.

Students involved with problem-based learning are using those quintessential, 21st-century competencies required for their burgeoning roles in a technologically advanced world (i.e., self-awareness, collaboration, constructivist thinking, effective use of technology, and distributed cognition; see figure 6.2).

## A Word of Caution about Problem-Based Learning

Problem-based learning does not come without its challenges. Many of the critiques of problem-based learning discuss the abstract nature of problem-based learning. For instance, problem development and students' self-direction are aspects that are both incredibly context dependent, subjective, and unpredictable.

Many teachers are concerned not only about the level of independence required, but also about the level of abstract reasoning, cognitive demand, and self-regulation required of students in order to be successful in problem-based classrooms. Perhaps this is the primary reason why the problem-based approach to instruction has traditionally been reserved for middle grades and secondary students.

However, a possible suggestion toward minimizing the degree of unpredictability (besides simply embracing it as an aspect of problem-based learning) is for teachers to model and clearly define the procedure (i.e., the objective, students' roles, instructional resources, and so on) via shorter or more discrete units of study. Once teachers feel that students have the foundation necessary to resolve problems with efficiency and appropriateness, they will be able to delve into more rigorous and extended tasks and assessments.

## What Is Project-Based Learning?

Whereas problem-based learning asks teachers and students to design, define, and resolve personally relevant problems, project-based learning presents students with an opportunity to resolve complex, content-driven questions, problems, or challenges. Sometimes referred to as *product-based learning*, project-based learning provides a vehicle by which teachers can intentionally design learning outcomes within the context of a content area or field of study. Project-based learning often serves as the ideal constructivist-oriented instructional strategy as it responds to many of the instructional and assessment challenges presented within problem-based learning. For example, the sometimes vague and abstract aspects of problem-based learning are abated. With project-based learning, the objectives, methods, assessments, and presentation modalities are outlined and explained. Concerns about students' abilities to self-regulate are mollified because students learn to self-regulate via the outlines and guidance of their teachers.

Over the remainder of the project's duration, the teacher serves as an instructional resource—providing essential materials, tools, and even remediation and enrichment as necessary. The culmination of the project-based learning cycle is an opportunity to share or present the final product. Assessment of the project typically happens with the assistance of an aligned, teacher-made rubric, which students use as information about their critical-thinking and problem-solving competencies.

For teachers interested in going deeper into the components of project-based learning, see the book *Work That Matters: A Teacher's Guide to Project-Based Learning* (2012) by Alec Patton. He covers the three keys to successful projects: (a) exhibition, (b) multiple drafts, and (c) critique. In addition to the structure that these tasks add to the learning cycle, each of these tasks also adds to the level of performance and impacts the quality of students' final products.

## What Is Performance-Based Learning?

Although performance-based learning is not a new approach to interdisciplinary instruction, its use as the primary vehicle for creative and self-directed learning certainly is. What makes performance-based learning (and assessment) so appealing to educators, especially in the era of 21st-century technologies, is that it offers a framework by which educators can offer students opportunities to acquire and apply knowledge, skills, and work habits that they need in order to be successful (Hibbard et al., 1996).

Because the goal of performance-based learning is to integrate knowledge and application competencies, performance-based learning identifies and requires several keys components within the performance task to facilitate the process.

**Component 1: Background.** This section of the performance task generally provides the standard or learning target, but presented within the context of a lived or relatable example from which students can make personal connections.

**Component 2: Task and Purpose.** The goal of this component is to provide students with specific information regarding the objective, or final product, expected upon the completion of the task. The task is uniquely designed to enable students to make personal connections to, or apply background knowledge of the standard. The task provides a rationalized purpose for its completion—whether implied or overtly stated.

**Component 3: Audience.** The audience refers to the intended reviewers and recipients of the completed product. The students' awareness of the audience is key to setting the purpose for learning and for mediating students' self-regulation, as it enables learners to see the impact of their work.

**Component 4: Procedure.** This element of PBL includes the intermediate tasks to be completed that are naturally embedded within the task in order to complete it. It does not explicate *how* students are to go about completing the task, but instead provides some provisions on how students can begin and proceed through the stages of the task until it is completed (see the next section for Dr. Bryson's adaptation of a performance task used with fifth grade).

Each of these components aligns with the development and mastery of the 21st-century skills previously discussed (refer back to figures 6.1 and 6.2). The inclusion of the *background*, or contextual situation for which the strand applies, aligns with building students' self-awareness, critical reflection, and global and cultural responsiveness. The *task*, and the purpose embedded within the task, respond to the previously mentioned student factors, as well as the constructivist competencies because of students' use of reasoning, critical thinking, and problem solving throughout the process of completing the performance task.

In addition to the self-regulatory benefits of having an *audience*, the inclusion of an audience corresponds with the collaborative, as well as globally and culturally responsive, skills required to embody the social and cross-cultural awareness, accountability, and responsibility necessitated by an audience.

The steps included within the *procedural* element of the performance task enables students to employ as well as take advantage of the constructivist, collaborative, and media and technological opportunities and tools available to them. It would appear that performance-based learning provides an ideal and timely response by which educators can prepare and assess 21st-century learners for their future roles in the global marketplace.

## Example of a Performance Task: Inventions Performance Task

### Background

Living in the 19th century was rough! There were no phones or electricity and none of the advances in modern medical science like we see today (nope, no plant-based zit creams!). Fortunately, during the early 20th century, there were some ingenious pioneers who saw beyond themselves to create inventions that proved to help all of mankind (e.g., the Wright brothers, George Washington Carver, Alexander Graham Bell, and Thomas Edison)!

Fast-forward 100 years. The inhabitants of the 21st century (yep, this means you) are still dealing with absences in, and glitches with, their modern-day technologies.

Now it is your turn to pioneer an invention and make your mark on the world like so many of the brilliant pioneers before you. Who knows? You may offer the answer to a problem that 22nd-century inhabitants won't ever know existed!

### Task and Purpose

*Task 1.* Create an invention that you think will benefit someone or something in our 21st-century lives. Be as creative as you can. You must create a model of the invention (Note: The model does not have to work).

*Task 2.* You must describe your invention in great detail by way of a written paper. Be very specific about the purpose of the invention. Make sure that you explain why your invention is important and how it will change society.

*Audience*

You will present an explanation of your invention to the class, attending parents, and our STEM business partners. Your presentation will be at least five minutes long, and your audience will be permitted to ask you questions.

*Procedure*

Task 1. Model of Your Invention

1. Your model should be large enough for the class to see it when you give your presentation, but small enough to carry on the bus.
2. Remember that the invention must be a positive contribution to people, animals, and/or the environment.
3. Details and creativity are key expectations for this part of the performance task.
4. Remember that the final product must be neat, imaginative, and professional.

Task 2. Written Explanation of Your Invention

1. Your essay must be typed, double-spaced, Times New Roman (font style), and in size 12 font.
2. Although this is not a formal essay, your writing should reflect that you'd want someone to read your work.
3. Ensure that your paper answers the following questions: What is it? What does it do? Why is it important? What will it replace (if anything)? How and why will you use it? How would it improve someone's or something's life? When and where will it be used? What ways will this invention change or affect our lives?

Lesson adapted from http://www.wallkillcsd.k12.ny.us/education/projects/projects.php?sectionid=10832&

## PBL³ Assessment

Generally, the method by which problem-, project-, and performance-based tasks are evaluated is via a rubric—those observational tools that provide categorical, or domain specific, evaluations, as well as scoring information that is subsequently used to tabulate a numeric score or letter grade (see table 6.3 for an example of a rubric for a performance task).

Another, more flexible, variation to the rubric as the method of performance-task assessment was offered by Hibbard and colleagues (1996). This modified assessment approach is known as the *Performance Task Assess-*

**Table 6.3.    Traditional Rubric for the Inventions Performance Task**

| | 4 | 3 | 2 | 1 |
|---|---|---|---|---|
| **Originality and Usefulness of This Invention** | This invention is very creative, shows a great deal of originality, and could be quite useful. | This invention is creative, shows originality, and could be useful. | This invention is a springboard or variation of something that has already been invented. | This invention appeared to be thrown together at the last minute, and it is evident that very little thought was put into it. |
| **Name of Invention** | The name for this invention is very clever and creative. It is apparent that the student put a great deal of thought into it. | The name for this invention is clever and creative. It is apparent that the student spent time thinking of this name. | The name for this invention is somewhat clever or creative. | The name of the invention seems as if the student hurriedly came up with it. |
| **Diagram or Blueprint of Invention** | The diagram or blueprint is very detailed, with all parts of the invention clearly labeled. | The diagram or blueprint has some detail, and most parts of the invention are clearly labeled. | The diagram or blueprint has very little detail and few of the parts of the invention are clearly labeled. | The diagram or blueprint was not turned in. The diagram or blueprint was hurriedly drawn. |
| **Expository Rough Draft for This Invention** | Student's rough draft is thoroughly edited, revised, and ready to be published. | Student's rough draft has been edited and revised. | Student's rough draft has been partially edited and revised. | Student's rough draft has very little editing and/or revising. Student did not turn in the rough draft. |
| **Presentation** | Student demonstrates full knowledge by answering all class questions with explanations and elaboration. | Student is at ease with expected answers to all questions, without elaboration. | Student is uncomfortable with information and is able to answer only basic questions. | Student does not have grasp of information; student cannot answer questions about subject. |

*ment List*, which provides a set list of items and skill competencies that the student must complete in order to demonstrate mastery of the topic or theme. According to Hibbard and colleagues (1996), performance-task lists provide students with the structure that they need to work independently, while encouraging them to attend to and improve the quality of their work.

Assessment lists also enable the teacher to efficiently provide students with information regarding the strengths and weaknesses of their work (Hibbard et al., 1996, p. 8; see figure 6.4). Another feature of assessment lists is that it requires self-assessment of the students' ability to meet each of the requirements in addition to the teacher's assessment. Discrepancies between scores are discussed and revisions are made based on the conclusions of those discussions.

Although both of these options (i.e., rubrics and performance-task assessment lists) offer more efficient methods and performance ranges for students' level of proficiency, flaws of subjectivity, domain validity, and the embedded inhibition of student growth can exist. These problems might occur because in PBL[3] (a) the teacher ultimately determines the final grade and (b) once the grade has been assigned, students can perceive that the learning cycle ends. Therefore, teachers might want to consider the use of alternative methods of grading and assessment. These will be discussed in greater detail, shortly.

| | Points Possible | Earned Assessment | |
| --- | --- | --- | --- |
| | | Self | Teacher |
| **Invention Project** | | | |
| 1. There is a creative model present. | | | |
| 2. The model meets the size requirements. | | | |
| 3. The invention meets a 21st-century need. | | | |
| 4. The invention positively affects society. | | | |
| 5. Time and care was given to create the product. | | | |
| 6. The model is neat, imaginative, and professional. | | | |
| **Written Portion** | | | |
| 1. The paper meets the formatting guidelines. | | | |
| 2. The paper is well-written (readability). | | | |
| 3. The paper responds to each of the prompts as required. | | | |
|   a. What is it? | | | |
|   b. What does it do? | | | |
|   c. Why is it important? | | | |
|   d. What will it replace (if anything)? | | | |
|   e. How and why would you use it? | | | |
|   f. How would it improve someone's or something's life? | | | |
|   g. When and where will it be used? | | | |
|   h. What ways will this invention affect our lives? | | | |

**Figure 6.4.** Performance task assessment list for the inventions performance task.

## A Final Note Regarding PBL³

It is important to note that PBL³ is not an instructional approach intended to usurp the traditional forms of instruction and assessment (i.e., there is no need to throw out your favorite lessons or units!). It is these traditional approaches that enable educators to ensure that students can demonstrate knowledge via recalling, identifying, and illustrating ideas and content because this serves as the precursor to applying the ideas in more rigorous contexts.

However, if the instructional aim or learning objective requires higher-order thinking skills such as classifying, investigating, evaluating, or creating new ideas and concepts, then reworking those favorite lessons and units into the PBL format may be the more viable approach to facilitate that skill development.

## Other Assessments That Gauge 21st-Century Learning

In chapter 4, several approaches to instructive assessments that lend themselves to the teaching of 21st-century competencies were reviewed. For example, the significance of *before-learning* assessments was illustrated via the use of the strategies like Brain Dump or No Voices. There were also rigorous strategies to assess students' knowledge during learning (e.g., Error Analysis, Three Heads Together, Stand Up Review).

In the current chapter, the value of rubrics, checklists, and nongraded formative feedback are discussed. While these and other approaches are all valid and meaningful methods of assessment for students, a novel approach to assessment that can also gauge students' 21st-century capabilities may be via cross-class, -school, or -country interactions and PBL³.

A vivid illustration of cross-country learning and evaluating came in the form of an *epals* project conducted by a middle-school class in suburban Atlanta, Georgia, and a school in Turku, Finland. The language arts teachers at both schools met through an online global learning community called epals (https://www.epals.com). By connecting with students in Finland, there was the added benefit of communicating in English since Finnish students have English classes from early childhood.

The teachers set up a writing exchange for the students where they had to document the types of activities that they did during their day. Each Finnish student was paired with one American student. What made the project interesting was that the first sets of communication among the pairs were only via email. The students got to know each other strictly through their written communication. The writing partners assessed each other's writing with rubrics that focused on topic content and reader engagement.

As a grand finale for the epals project, the student partners got to virtually see each other and talk face-to-face. The students found out that preconceived ideas about the other person were different when you cannot see any physical aspects of the person. The project unintentionally led to some open and honest discussion about how people should judge others more by their thinking and actions than their physical appearance.

If you have not considered cross-class, -school, or -country learning tasks, consider giving it a try. You can find numerous global projects online. One site you might find helpful is called Connect All Schools (http://www.connectallschools.org/).

## Concerns about Grading: Revisited

Despite the number and variety of assessment resources that have been provided throughout this text, a lingering concern for teachers who use these various tools, especially with regard to PBL, is: "How can I effectively and appropriately grade student work that involves intangible processes (i.e., communication, interdisciplinary content mastery, technological awareness and use, and the like) as well as students' final products?" Well, there is good news!

A teacher can experience a refreshing challenge by taking a bold leap into a nontraditional approach to assessment. This can be experienced by considering a break from the traditional method of assigning grades to a more collaborative and restorative practice of supplying narrative feedback throughout the course of the learning cycle.

One of the most critical elements to feedback during PBL[3]-type tasks is formative feedback on drafts of the projects. When assigning a project, chunk it into discrete parts and assign a checklist or rubric for each portion along the way. Students or groups turn in drafts of each chunk. The key is giving specific feedback about what is going well and what needs improvement.

Sometimes peer assessment can be used effectively if peers are given very specific criteria that indicate precise expectations. Peers can look over the drafts and search for the expected criteria. Some teachers have found the use of highlighter pens helpful so that peers can highlight the elements of the draft that are representative of the criteria.

In his book *Assessment 3.0: Throw Out Your Grade Book and Inspire Learning* (2015), Mark Barnes strongly recommends narrative feedback. Barnes endorses this type of performance assessment, not only because of its ability to encourage growth and proficiency *during* the formative assessment process, but also because it negates many of the counterproductive effects often experienced with traditional forms of numeric and traditional grading systems, such as time constraints, subjectivity, and lack of student motivation.

However, with narrative feedback grading, the teacher and student share reflections on and perceptions about the work that has been completed over the course of the marking period. These reflections include thoughtful debriefings, surveys of progress, and standards-based conversations that enable both parties to discuss, with an astute awareness, the student's level of proficiency in relation to the course's prescribed learning objectives (Barnes, 2015).

With narrative feedback, the emphasis is placed on the value of learning as a process—not only the numerical score or letter grade achieved. Narrative feedback restores students' sense of ownership of the content, which is transferable to other contexts and enables students to understand what *they* can intentionally do to improve their own level of proficiency.

What is brilliant about this formula is that it gets at the heart of what *true* teaching and learning actually is *in situ*. It helps students see where they are along the continuum of mastery, while empowering them to independently act in order to supplement and extend their current degree of proficiency.

If educators desire for students to truly engage in the *process* of learning, it may be a worthwhile consideration for educators to remove the obstacle that impedes the process—numerical scores and other subjective and traditional approaches to grading. If teachers feel that they've already lost their students, consider narrative feedback to reignite students' interest and involve them in collaborative conversations about their own learning.

## WHAT SHOULD YOU DO IF YOUR LOCAL SCHOOL OR DISTRICT REQUIRES TRADITIONAL GRADES?

It would be unfortunate if, after all the hard work of planning performance tasks and evaluating students via narrative feedback or some other method of constant comparative assessment, all of the students' learning outcomes were simply reduced to an *A*, a 76%, or a check mark.

Unfortunately, this is an issue that many educators often face—especially in the era of high-stakes testing and other measures of accountability (see chapter 2). So what can teachers do if, at the end of the day, numeric scores and letter grades remain tantamount to formative and summative methods of feedback? Consider employing the following protocol to garner support for collaborative grading efforts:

1. Communicate with your administrators about the undesirable effects of traditional grading on students' processes of learning;
2. Articulate the potential positive effects of narrative feedback—especially students obtaining the skill of critical analysis of their own

work, which will aid them when they are differentiating between and responding to formative and summative assessments;

3. Offer standards-based grading through which students' longitudinal performance (e.g., online portfolios, response trends, or catalogued verbal responses), or what Barnes (2015) calls *performance reviews*, are employed to collaboratively evaluate with students their progress in relation to the learning target;

4. Offer to make responsive adjustments to (or discontinue) the practice of narrative-feedback grading at the end of the marking period if comparative, common (i.e., grade level or department) assessments indicate a deficit via reduced class performance.

It is our fervent hope that this chapter on 21st-century learning and assessment has provided, at the very least, a foundation and framework by which to cultivate constructivist and critically pedagogical classrooms. Without this classroom shift to more authentic, performance-based methods of learning, students are left bereft of the skills that they would need in order to be critical problem solvers, as well as globally and culturally responsive.

## POST-READING QUESTIONS

The questions are first listed for readers to contemplate on their own. Additionally, the questions are listed a second time with commentary from the authors' perspectives:

1. How can assessment be responsive to the instructional needs of 21st-century learners?
2. What underlying beliefs about teaching and learning promote a forward-thinking approach to the design and implementation of assessment strategies?
3. What types of assignments and assessments best measure and promote the skills needed for learners of the future?
4. How can educators embrace and utilize technological tools to enhance 21st-century teaching and learning?
5. What can educators do to promote the implementation of 21st-century assignments and assessments?

## POST-READING QUESTIONS

**How can assessment be responsive to the instructional needs of 21st-century learners?** Throughout this chapter, we have focused on the theme of envisioning new ways to implement assessments that promote futuristic views of learning. One might wonder . . . when the 22nd century arrives on January 1, 2101, will schools still be using the same archaic assessments that are currently in place? It's an interesting question to ponder. It seems hard enough to imagine the broad level of systemic changes that will be needed to make assessments meaningful and relevant to students living in the 21st century.

What is clear is that for assessment to be responsive, it must first be relevant to learning needs. Many might argue about the ways to define those learning needs. Others might think more broadly about the goals of education. Many educational experts say that education's goal is to support students in developing the skills, concepts, and dispositions that will help them be responsible and contributing members of society. With these goals in mind, we will all have to think about our current assessments. Our educational system has been fairly effective at assessing skills, but not so competent in assessing concepts and dispositions.

**What underlying beliefs about teaching and learning promote a forward-thinking approach to the design and implementation of assessment strategies?** A thought-provoking word that is rarely used when talking about beliefs is the term *epistemology*. Epistemology is a branch of philosophy concerned with the nature of knowing. Occasionally, it is very instructive to reflect on your core beliefs about teaching, learning, and assessment. For example, a teacher whose epistemology is grounded in constructivist theory is going to have a different way of knowing than a teacher who is more aligned to traditional behavioristic views about teaching.

Figure 6.1 shows our beliefs about the factors that make up the assessment proficiencies required of 21st-century teachers (i.e., pedagogical beliefs and values, instructional approaches, and assessment types). It is always a good thing for teachers to take some time to reflect on the beliefs they hold. These core principles ultimately impact the way teachers design classroom assessment and utilize school and state-mandated assessments. The pervasive element behind all of these factors is the teachers' beliefs or epistemology. This might be a good time to reflect on your core beliefs and the way they impact your actions and reactions.

**What types of assignments and assessments best measure and promote the skills needed for learners of the future?** In this chapter, we have tried to make the case for assignments that promote deeper levels of thinking. As shown in the discussion on distributed cognition, students can access basic facts in a matter of moments via the Internet. Students' recall of low-level procedural or factual information is not the type of skills needed for 21st-century careers. With these issues in mind, educators must consider how to design, implement, and assess deeper-level tasks such as the examples we presented in the section of this chapter related to PBL[3].

Instructional tasks need to be designed and assessed so that students are given a wide span of opportunities to show how they use their minds to research, think critically, collaborate effectively, and analyze outcomes. And yes, these types of tasks are more time consuming to create and evaluate. It is much easier to give a multiple-choice assessment than evaluate a complex performance-based task. However, we believe it is well worth the effort in the long run.

**How can educators embrace and utilize technological tools to enhance 21st-century teaching and learning?** As of the writing of this book, it is over 16 years into the 21st century and technological progress has been pretty amazing. There is now global access to the Internet and smartphones abound, even for elementary school children. Most technology experts see the progress of technology as an upward spiral. It seems schools are the ones lagging behind.

School leaders and policymakers must come to terms with this technological explosion. Equipment must be brought up-to-date. Schools and communities have to find ways to bridge the digital divide that prevents some students and families from online access.

Teachers should be encouraged to learn new technologies and expected to implement electronic tools as part of their instructional strategies. Professional learning must be a part of the solution. Teachers need opportunities to experiment and be learners.

All of these solutions take time, money, and will power. We all need to rise to the occasion. One of the best advocacy organizations for effective instructional technology integration is the International Society for Technology in Education (ISTE). We highly recommend that educators learn more about this organization and join their efforts to bring education into the 21st century. See more about ISTE at http://www.iste.org.

**What can educators do to promote the implementation of 21st-century assignments and assessments?** We believe that the best way that teachers can promote innovate strategies is to try them out and perform some level of action research to show that they are making a difference. What is most frustrating is for educational advocates and reformers to make suggestions and have them immediately turned away. A 21st-century educator has to be open to try new techniques and methods in order to accommodate the changing needs of students.

Administrators, especially, need to give teachers some autonomy in creating a school climate that opens the way for some level of experimentation with new classroom assessment. If educators have students as their top priority and number one focus, promoting the techniques outlined in this chapter should be welcomed. If the strategies don't work, that is fine, try something else.

## CHAPTER NOTES: PARTNERSHIP FOR 21ST-CENTURY SCHOOLS

According to the Partnership for 21st-Century Schools (2011, http://www.p21.org/), learners must demonstrate proficiency of the following capabilities in order to be successful:

- *Core Content Knowledge and Knowledge of 21st-Century Interdisciplinary Themes*, by which schools "promote an understanding of academic content at much higher levels [of rigor] by weaving 21st-century interdisciplinary themes [e.g., global awareness, financial, economic, business, entrepreneurial literacy, and environmental literacy] into the core subjects" of English language arts, mathematics, science, and social studies.
- *Learning and Innovative Capabilities*, which include skills related to creativity and innovation, critical thinking, and problem solving, as well as foster communicative and collaborative capabilities.
- *Information, Media, and Technological Skills*, which relate to students' exhibition of a range of functional and critical-thinking skills.
- *Life and Career Skills*, which include flexibility and adaptability, initiative and self-direction, social and cross-cultural skills, productivity and accountability, and leadership and responsibility (Partnership for 21st-Century Schools, 2011, p. 2).

### Additional Recommended Readings

Henriksen, D., Mishra, P., & Fisser, P. (2016). Infusing creativity and technology in 21st-century education: A systemic view for change. *Journal of Educational Technology & Society, 19*(3), 27–37.

Spector, J., Ifenthaler, D., Sampson, D., Yang, L., Mukama, E., Warusavitarana, A., & Gibson, D. (2016). Technology enhanced formative assessment for 21st-century learning. *Journal of Educational Technology & Society, 19*(3), 58–71.

Svihla, V., Vye, N., Brown, M., Phillips, R., Gawel, D., & Bransford, J. (2009). Interactive learning assessments for the 21st century. *Education Canada, 49*(3), 44–47.

## REFERENCES

Barnes, M. (2015). *Assessment 3.0: Throw out your grade book and inspire learning.* Thousand Oaks, CA: Corwin.

Brooks, J. G., & Brooks, M. G. (1999). *In search of understanding: The case for constructivist classrooms.* Alexandria, VA: ASCD.

Carr, S., Johnson, N., & Bush, L. (2016). Distributed cognition: Teachers' perceptions and implications for learning outcomes and instructional technology. In C. X. Wang (Ed.), *Handbook of research on learning outcomes and learning opportunities in the digital age* (pp. 152–179). Hershey, PA: IGI Global.

Cleary, T. J., & Zimmerman, B. J. (2004). Self-regulation empowerment program: A school-based program to enhance self-regulated and self-motived cycles of student learning. *Psychology in the Schools, 41*(5), 537–550.

Costa, A., & Kallick, B. (2008). *Learning and leading with habits of mind.* Alexandria, VA: ASCD.

Freire, P. (2000). *Pedagogy of the oppressed.* (M. B. Ramos, Trans.). New York, NY: Blooms-bury. (Original work published 1970).

Hall, J. (2016). *Mathematics education technology.* Retrieved from http://www.mathedtech.pbworks.com

Hibbard, K. M., Van Wagenen, L., Lewbel, S., Waterbury-Wyatt, S., Shaw, S., Pelletier, K., . . . Wislocki, J.A. (1996). *Performance-based learning and assessment.* Alexandria, VA: ASCD.

Hutchins, E. (1995). *Cognition in the wild.* Cambridge, MA: MIT Press.

Kagan, S. (2013). *Cooperative learning: Structures.* San Clemente, CA: Kagan Publishing.

Ladson-Billings, G. (1994). *The dream keepers.* San Francisco, CA: Jossey-Bass.

Patton, A. (2012). *Work that matters: A teacher's guide to project-based learning.* London, UK: Paul Hamlyn Foundation. Retrieved from http://www.innovationunit.org/sites/default/files/Teacher's%20Guide%20to%20Project-based%20Learning.pdf

Pea, R. D. (1993). Distributed intelligence and designs for education. In G. Salomon (Ed.), *Distributed cognitions: Psychological and educational considerations* (p. 47–87). Cambridge, UK: Cambridge University Press.

Schunk, D. H. (2012). *Learning theories: An educational perspective.* Boston, MA: Allyn & Bacon.

Stanford University. (2001). Problem-based learning. *Speaking of Teaching, 11*(1), Retrieved from http://web.stanford.edu/dept/CTL/cgi-bin/docs/newsletter/problem_based_learning.pdf

Wink, J. (2011). *Critical pedagogy: Notes from the real world* (4th ed.). Upper Saddle River, NJ: Pearson.

# Index

# About the Authors

**Sherah Betts Carr**, PhD, has worked in the P–12 educational arena for more than 35 years, teaching numerous grade levels and serving in leadership positions. As well as teaching students, she has taught educators, led a school professional learning program, and presented more than 125 workshops in the metro Atlanta area. Sherah is an associate professor at Mercer University–Tift College of Education in Atlanta, in the master's and doctoral programs, primarily teaching courses related to curriculum, instruction, and assessment. Sherah has presented at numerous state, regional, and national conferences. She also leads a professional learning and research project with teachers in the Dominican Republic.

**Anaya L. Bryson**, PhD, has been an elementary education teacher with Gwinnett County public schools for more than 10 years—teaching numerous grade levels and providing instructional support for English-language learners, students with disabilities, and students within gifted education programs. Anaya has served as an instructional lead teacher and has conducted numerous professional development workshops for teachers regarding the response to intervention process, differentiated instruction for gifted students, and best practices in mathematics. Her research interests include critically and culturally reflective pedagogy, mathematics education, self and teacher efficacy, and professionally developing novice teachers.

Made in the USA
Lexington, KY
12 July 2017